A MAN & HIS MEATBALLS

A MAN & HIS MEATBALLS

The Hilarious but True Story of a Self-Taught Chef and Restaurateur

WITH 75 RECIPES

JOHN LaFEMINA

WITH PAM MANELA

REGAN

An Imprint of HarperCollinsPublishers

Our daughter, Tess, samples her first meatball at eleven months.

To my wife and best friend, Pam—

For your love, humor, support, and grasp of the English language.

You brought my stories to life in this book,

and I could not have done it without you.

To my daughter, Tess—

For amazing me every day, keeping me grounded,

and being ridiculously cute.

I love you both.

CONTENTS

GRABBING LIFE BY THE MEATBALLS

~

One

MY BACK STORY

THE DAY BEFORE Ápizz opened in September 2002, I walked down Eldridge Street obsessing over whether or not it would all come together in time. Would the trained but untested staff know to recommend the Montepulciano d'Abruzzo with the meatballs? Was there too much Parmigiano in the braised wild boar lasagna? Were the amber gels I wrapped around the dining room lights making the room too orange? Would anyone even show up, and, most important, would they like the food?

These were the things I felt I could, to some extent, control. But as I got closer to the restaurant, I saw that something was so out of place, I stopped dead in my tracks. "What the hell is this?" I thought. There on the street, a few feet from the door of my brand-new restaurant, was a phone booth, completely ruining the beautiful and carefully designed entrance, which I had finally gotten right. I had spent weeks scouring lumber yards from Coney Island to the Bronx for the perfect piece of mahogany for the front door, and now it was blocked by this ugly phone booth. I didn't know how or exactly when it got there—it wasn't in the ground when I left the restaurant at two A.M. the night before—but it was the last thing I needed in front of my place. Phone booths on the Lower East Side meant kids hanging out, and my little stretch of Eldridge Street was scary enough without that.

3

As a native of Canarsie, Brooklyn, I'd become something of an expert at identifying scams and get-rich-quick schemes, and this felt like one right off the bat. I knew something was wrong with a company installing a phone booth between two A.M. and eight A.M. The name written across the top may as well have been "Joe's Bogus Phone Company."

The first thing I did was call my cousin Tally, who works security for Verizon, and explained the situation. He had heard of these phone booths popping up in the middle of the night, usually next to bodegas in neighborhoods where people wouldn't complain. This time they were wrong. I remained completely calm and did the only rational thing there was to do: I ran down to the local hardware store.

"I need a jackhammer," I said.

I rented a fifty-pound jackhammer and brought it back to Eldridge Street. I ran an extension cord out of the restaurant to the street and plugged it in. I jumped on it like a pogo stick and pounded it into the pavement for hours in the hot summer sun, slowly unbolting this metal monstrosity from my sidewalk as the neighborhood kids cheered me on. Two of these kids, my porter, and I hauled the phone booth down the street and dumped it in an empty lot. I still had a long list of things to do to get ready for the opening, so I got back to work.

End of story, right? Wrong. The next day—opening day—I pulled up to Eldridge Street in a taxi. I thought I was dreaming. The phone booth was back.

I went back to the hardware store, the vein in my right temple pumping overtime. This time I bought the jackhammer. When I detached the phone booth from the sidewalk again, I didn't hide it in a lot down the street. I left it lying there on its side, in front of my place, a sort of *message* to the people who put it back up in the middle of the night. And about a minute later, one of those people—a tall forty-something guy in a dark suit—was standing next to me, his company's phone booth lying at his feet.

This guy actually tried to intimidate me with that double-talk code that wannabes use. He said I obviously didn't know who he was "with" or who the officers of his company were. I told him to have his CEO call my CEO and while he was at it, ask around and find out who *I'm* with. As he walked away, my wife, who witnessed the whole thing, asked me who in fact it was that I was *with*. I shrugged and said, "You."

$\sim$

I WOULD SAY, on average, about six people a week tell me their dream is to open a restaurant. I just nod and smile because I was once one of them and, more often than not, I know exactly what prompted this fantasy. These future restaurateurs are usually stuck in a career they can't stand—accountant, lawyer, some bad tech job, ad sales—love to bake or cook at home, and have been told one too many times that they throw the best dinner parties ever. They believe that if their in-laws and friends enjoy their food and hosting skills, so will the discriminating diners of New York. But most important, these people believe that opening a restaurant will be a fun and profitable alternative to their current jobs and lives. And maybe it will be. It all depends on them.

Here's the deal: owning a restaurant is a life change, not a career change. That's the biggest thing to remember. And when I say *owning,* I mean doing whatever it takes to stay alive—getting in before everyone else arrives and staying until the end of the night, sitting in every seat in the dining room every day to make sure the music is at a perfect volume, the air conditioner is hitting each table just right, and the view of the kitchen is unobstructed. It means attending to every detail. Financing a restaurant is an entirely different thing, and we'll get to that later.

I have never understood why people say they want to open a restaurant when they retire, like it's an easy thing to do later in life. That's like me saying I want to be a construction worker or ditchdigger when I turn sixty-five. If budding restaurateurs understand and are ready to embrace the blood, sweat, and tears that come along with the life, they just might have a shot.

More likely than not, this person with restaurant dreams is what I call a *Saturday Nighter,* someone who walks into my restaurant on a busy Saturday night, catches a glimpse of Jessica Simpson or Diane Sawyer in the dining room, and thinks the restaurant business is nothing but glamour, schmoozing, and money. The week we opened Ápizz, my friends and family read about it in *New York* magazine and the *New York Times.* When they came in for dinner on opening night and saw every table full, they announced with all honesty that I had a hit on my hands.

My old friends from high school are all Saturday Nighters, especially Joey Cantalupalini. The first month we were open, Joey, a short bulldog of a guy with a gold Christ head dangling from his neck, called to say he got a babysitter and was driving to the city from Staten Island. He walked in, noticed a table filled with young women, and pulled me aside to say,

"Man, we should have done this years ago." *We,* I thought to myself. Then I just laughed, wishing he could have seen me thirty minutes before service when I was unclogging the toilet and running to two different Whole Foods markets looking for heirloom tomatoes. I wondered if Joey would like to help the next time I had to pull a phone booth out of the ground.

Now that I have had lots of phone booth days—and great ones, too—under my belt, plenty of people want to talk to me about opening their own restaurants. I can tell they think I might know some secret. That's how it works; you do one thing right and everyone thinks you're the expert. On the other hand, if you do one thing wrong, you're a moron. You're only as good as your last meal.

I don't have all the answers. I don't know why the restaurant on the corner of Sixth Street and Second Avenue isn't making it, but the place across the street with worse food is booming. I don't have a clue why diners will have no problem paying fifteen dollars for a martini but will complain that a fourteen-dollar pizza is too expensive. And I can't explain why my Mexican busboy, who makes a couple of hundred dollars a week, is asking his fiancée to sign a prenup. What I do know are the answers for my restaurant. I know how to make it better, and I know what will make my customers come back for more.

Years ago, when I decided to open my restaurant, I met a few guys who were planning on doing the same thing. They all had elaborate plans that involved highly researched concepts, number crunching, and large spaces. As someone who got his most useful schooling on the streets of Brooklyn, I didn't come from this world. Terms like *sales projections* and *pie charts* are about as foreign to me as Japanese. And to this day, it's one of the things I'm most thankful for. It has forced me to use common sense, and that has served me well.

In fact, using common sense is one of the most important things about the entire process. (If you're interested in opening a restaurant and you're the kind of person who needs a nice, bound business plan with lots of charts and graphics, a team of investors, and a rule book, you should stop reading this right now, because this book is not for you.) Break your plan down to the simplest form of common sense: when looking for a space and figuring out how much rent you can afford, ask yourself, "How many meatballs or plates of grilled fish, and glasses of wine do I have to serve to simply pay the rent?" If you have to serve a minimum of two hundred people a night at forty dollars a head just to get by and the restaurant you're looking at only seats fifty, you may want to rethink your choice of location. Or else, be damn sure of what you're getting yourself into.

Here's the bottom line. The number of tables and the number of hours in which you'll serve food are pretty much fixed. If two people sit down at a two-top at six o'clock, they'll occupy that table for an hour and a half to two hours. Two more people walk in at, let's say, eight o'clock and dine at the same table for the next two hours. And, in this perfect scenario, two more people come in at ten o'clock to bring your total number of turnovers for the evening to three. Since you probably can't produce more tables and you definitely can't make people want to sit down for dinner at eleven o'clock, you can figure out how many people your restaurant can accommodate when maxed out. Take that number and multiply it by your average price per head (to get this number, look at your menu and add up the price of an average appetizer, entrée, and glass of wine). You're probably looking at a pretty sweet number.

Now put the calculator down and come back to reality. In Manhattan, for example, nobody eats at six, no one shows up on time, and 10 percent of your reservations will be no-shows. So take your number and cut it in half. If you can make it on *this* number, you have a shot. Numbers don't lie. I never imagine the best case scenario or the worst case scenario; I need to feel comfortable with the middle ground. For me that's the smart move.

When I found the spot that now houses Ápizz, I figured I had to serve twenty-three people a night just to exist. The only thing out of the entire scenario that wouldn't change was the rent, so I made sure I felt comfortable with that number. If business is bad, you can lay off some of your help, order less wine, and adjust your costs accordingly to stay afloat. But try convincing your landlord to reduce your rent because business is slow—it's not happening.

Other important things to consider are the unforeseeable events that can affect your bottom line in a big way. If the Yankees are in the World Series, business is going to drop. If they're playing the Mets, you're completely screwed. So, if you're looking to spend thirty thousand a month just in rent, you better have a lot of money in the bank to cover your ass while business is bad. I prefer restaurants with low monthly numbers. If given the choice, I will always opt to spend more on the initial renovation and pay less each month to my landlord. If a blizzard hits the city three weekends in a row in January, I can cover my rent at Ápizz with no problem.

If this stuff scares you but you're still itching to be involved in the restaurant industry, you may want to consider forking over some money and being one of many investors in a project. Investors come and go as they please, eat for free, and can score tables for their friends on busy weekend nights. Most important, investors get to brag to everyone they know that they own a restaurant. It's usually all about ego, which is good because they rarely recoup their initial investment—lost money that won't make or break them. On the other hand, when you're an owner-operator, you essentially sell your soul to the restaurant, and the crazy thing is, you feel like you got the better end of the deal. For the owner-operator, getting back his money is not an option, it's an absolute necessity.

So you want to open a restaurant? The only thing I can tell you is *do it*. The *only* difference between me and you is that I did it. I leapt, for better or worse, head first like a high diver jumping off a cliff. All the other stuff, finding the right spot, the liquor license, hiring a good staff, will fall into place. If you have common sense and half a brain, you'll figure out those things. Just taking that initial leap is the hardest part. So stop sitting on the phone, talking about it with your friends, and researching the industry until you're blue in the face. Before you know it, you'll no longer have the money, the time, or worse, the guts. I refuse to let fear get in the way of some of the best experiences of my life.

As for all those guys with the researched concepts and pie charts eager to open up restaurants years ago? They're still planning.

From Bling-Bling to Braising

I STOOD BEHIND my counter at the New York Jewelry Exchange in November 1998, where I worked full time as a jeweler. My head was buried in a parcel filled with loose half-carat diamonds. I was working fast, trying to match enough D-colored stones for a tennis bracelet for a CEO's wife, who "needed it" for her weekend at Mar-a-Lago. I didn't really have time to deal with much else when Frank DeCarlo, a friend and chef at a local restaurant, came by to talk to me.

"What's up?" I said.

"Well, I'm trying to get my own restaurant going."

"Why are you coming to me?"

"I'm looking for about four or five investors," he said, handing me a copy of his business plan. "And I know you sell jewelry to a lot of big guys. I was hoping that you could pass this along to some of them."

"I don't know," I answered.

I took the plan and dropped it on my counter, without even glancing at its cover (you know how I feel about business plans). I asked him to tell me about his idea.

"It would be Italian, very authentic, but not a Mulberry Street kind of restaurant," he said. "I want the kitchen to have all open fires, no gas."

As he described the restaurant, I couldn't help but notice the excitement on his face. A thought occurred to me: what if I invested in it?

"Where?" I asked.

"Downtown, maybe the East Village or somewhere on the Bowery." I really liked both of those neighborhoods; they were cool yet still gritty and undeveloped.

"How much?" I said

"Three hundred and fifty thousand, maybe four hundred."

I had never really thought about investing in a restaurant before, but I really loved this idea—a stylish Italian restaurant, off the beaten path, rustic with lots of open flames; it sounded like a place where I would like to dine. Plus I had eaten at the East Village restaurant where Frank worked several times and knew he was a great cook. I thought he had a lot of talent and potential.

There was something about the whole thing that bothered me. If there were four or five investors, there would be too many cooks in the kitchen, so to speak, and I wouldn't want to be involved. I figured if I'm going to take a shot, I want a bigger piece of the pie. I quickly did the math in my head. I knew I had almost enough in the bank, and it wasn't doing much more than sitting there collecting 2 percent interest. I thought I could probably make some big jewelry deals over the next few months to cover the rest. It was a crazy gamble, but I was single, thirty-four years old, had no kids or major responsibilities, and something told me that this guy was a great bet. I said I would think about it.

After he left, I thumbed through his business plan and noticed a couple of bar charts and projected profits, all of which meant nothing to me. You're never going to see a business pitch with negative projections; they're always positive and usually off the mark. It wasn't the numbers I was interested in; it was Frank's idea and his potential as a chef that excited me. I tossed the plan in the trash. A week later, I committed to funding the entire operation.

Many restaurant owners and chefs go to cooking school, take over a family business, or have a lifelong passion to get into the industry. My segue into restaurants was much more random. After graduating from high school, I knew college was not in my future. To me, college meant nothing more than a four-year delay in what I wanted to do: have my own business. Before I became a jeweler, I job-hopped, hoping to find the business that was right for me.

I was eighteen years old when I got a job as a security guard at the New York Jewelry Exchange, a hectic, downtown marketplace open to the public, one of the last places of business in the city where people made deals on handshakes. My main responsibilities as a security guard were to walk around the selling floor and keep an eye on vendors' counters, where millions of dollars' worth of jewelry were shown to bargain-hungry customers. A couple of years later, I graduated from security detail and started working with a jeweler named Bobby Satin. Bobby had a pretty good business going, and the more I watched him in action—examining and buying diamonds, creating mammoth engagement rings—the more I thought I could be a good jeweler.

I immersed myself in the business, studying the many cuts and qualities of diamonds. I started designing my own pieces, looking for inspiration in history books and architecture. And I began to network, donating pieces for benefit auctions and giving away jewelry to models and celebrities, all for the sole purpose of getting photographed with them and impressing my and Bobby's regular customers. It all went a long way. I developed a nice customer base and slowly earned the trust of some of the city's biggest businessmen, who regularly bought stones from me for their wives and/or girlfriends. I also earned the respect of some of the most high-profile diamond dealers in the country, and eventually was able to buy a million dollars' worth of diamonds over the phone.

Most important, I was saving my money for something. I would be lying if I said I always knew I wanted to open a restaurant, because the truth is I had no idea. While I loved the fast pace of the Jewelry Exchange and dealing with precious gems, I had always felt that something was missing.

Less than one year after our first conversation about opening a restaurant, Frank and I walked into an old garage at 194 Elizabeth Street in downtown New York City, a place where locals went for oil changes and used parts. I immediately turned to him and said, "This is home."

From my mother to the owner of the building, not one person could believe we had actually signed a fifteen-year lease on such a run-down space in what was then an undesirable neighborhood. I took my life savings, every penny I had earned over the past twelve years at the Jewelry Exchange, and put it into renovating that Elizabeth Street space. It would later become a great cozy, yet sophisticated, restaurant called Peasant, a place I'm still proud of. To this day, what we did to that dilapidated garage still blows me away. But what I know now is that the perfect spot, rent, design, and neighborhood means nothing without great food. And at Peasant, that's what people keep coming back for: Frank's amazing cooking.

A few months into the renovation of Peasant, Frank hired a publicist named Pam Manela to handle the opening and essentially launch Peasant to the public and media. While my knowledge of PR was limited at the time, I knew it had something to do with celebrities, fabulous parties, and making sure the press wrote about both.

Peasant was still a construction site when I met Pam there in December 2000. It was my busy season at the Jewelry Exchange, so I only had about fifteen minutes or so for our meeting. We stood in the middle of what would be the dining room with our winter coats on while I talked for about ten minutes, offering my strong opinion on the kind of publicity I wanted for the restaurant—lots of Page Six mentions (the *New York Post*'s gossip column) and a big celebrity-filled opening party.

"I want this to be a hot spot," I said.

This publicist and I were clearly not on the same page. "I want it to be a hot spot, too, but I want to go about it in a different way," she said. "I would rather focus more heavily on the food than on the scene, build some integrity for the place." I just stood there and listened. I suddenly really wanted to score a date with her.

"If you're known for really good food, you'll have some staying power," she explained. "On the other hand, if you're the flavor of the month, you'll be out as quickly as you were in."

"I'm listening," I said.

"I can toss in a couple of gossip items here and there, but we shouldn't overdo it. We don't want to look like publicity whores."

By the end of our hour-long conversation I was hooked, both on this new strategy and our new publicist. For months, Pam and I had meetings and endless phone conversations on a regular basis. I couldn't help but notice the chemistry between us. She insisted she couldn't possibly date a client. I threatened to fire her.

A few months after Peasant opened, I managed to set up a "working dinner" with her at a romantic restaurant uptown, during which we talked about everything but work. Afterward we went to Opaline, a dimly lit lounge in the East Village, for a drink. It was there that I very suavely leaned into her by the bar and kissed her for the first time, her long dark hair spilling onto the bar top.

I was too busy kissing her to open my eyes, but suddenly I was aware of an undeniable burning smell. When I looked, I saw flames shooting out of the back of Pam's hair from a burning votive.

"Your hair is on fire," I said. Pam screamed. "We need water," I yelled to the bartender.

Pam and I at our wedding checking out the garnish
from the buffet . . . the head of a roasted suckling pig.

He grabbed his soda gun and quickly doused the back of her hair, putting out the flames. Thankfully, it looked a lot worse than it actually was, only a small patch of hair was singed. Afterward, she looked at me, smiled, and said, "That was hot." We were a couple from that moment on.

In the meantime, I worked at the Jewelry Exchange during the day and helped with the building of Peasant at night. The restaurant was nothing more than a business opportunity, but as the months of building turned into our first year of business, I could see that I wanted to be more involved; I needed more. The highlights of my career as a jeweler were those times when I designed a piece from scratch, really created something beautiful for someone to wear. I craved that same creative satisfaction at the restaurant.

One day, less than three years after Peasant's opening, I was sitting in my booth at the Jewelry Exchange thinking about the past few years. I had recently recouped my initial investment, and Peasant was doing well. I realized I wanted to open my own restaurant. Then I realized I couldn't wait to tell Pam my plan. I grabbed a pencil and pad and started sketching a dining room, and in the center a table with four chairs. As I added more details, the table top slowly transformed into the face of a ring, an emerald-cut stone surrounded by smaller emerald cuts in a platinum setting—understated and elegant, just like Pam. This ring would be perfect for her, I thought. I called her up and said, "Let's get married." She said, "Okay!" I picked out a stone for her. A few hours later, I started looking for a spot for my next restaurant.

Less than a year later, when Ápizz opened in early September 2002, I was still working at the Jewelry Exchange full time, Monday through Saturday until five o'clock. Afterward I would walk down the Bowery and over to Eldridge Street to arrive at Ápizz by five fifteen. I had a great manager, Xerxes Novoa, who I knew could really handle things without me being there every minute. I first met Xerxes, a Peruvian with a Greek name, when he was sixteen and a fitness trainer at a gym I belonged to. We kept in touch over the years and I always liked and trusted him. When, at twenty-six years old, he desperately wanted out of the corporate world and expressed interest in the restaurant industry, I offered him a job on the spot. Xerxes would lock up the restaurant at night, so, with me keeping my hours at the Jewelry Exchange, we had a pretty good system. In fact, everything was going fine until one hot October day, about a month after our grand opening, when I got a call from Xerxes.

"Yo, there's a crazy smell coming from the restaurant," he said. It was two o'clock, which meant we were opening in four hours.

"Where's it coming from?" I asked.

"I don't know, but it's bad."

"Can't you get rid of it? Turn on the fan or something," I said.

"I'm telling you it's the worst thing I have ever smelled in my life."

This was a really critical time for us. During the first few months, critics always show up unannounced and anonymously, so I rushed out of the Jewelry Exchange and ran to Ápizz to solve the problem before our first reservations arrived at six thirty. The smell hit me as soon as I turned the corner of Eldridge and Stanton. It was like a combination of everything you can imagine that's pungent, rotting in the hot sun. People on the street passed me with their shirts pulled up over their noses. This was not good.

Ápizz's front door was wide open, but the smell was a hundred times worse when I walked in, making me wince with misery. I went downstairs to the prep kitchen, the obvious source of the smell, to find Xerxes, fresh from throwing up, tossing over thirty pounds of spoiled fish into a large garbage bag. It seemed that our brand new refrigerators, which held all of our fish, had broken down in the middle of the night, giving twenty pounds of striped bass, seven pounds of calamari, and nine pounds of skate plenty of time to fester.

I called the supplier that sold us the faulty fridge and demanded that a new one be delivered within the hour. Thankfully, the Bowery, the street that houses most of the city's restaurant-supply companies, is only a couple of blocks away from Ápizz. In the meantime, Xerxes and I had to get rid of the rotten fish and the broken refrigerator immediately. You don't simply throw out thirty-six pounds of bad fish. The strongest garbage bag in the world was no match for this smell, so we couldn't just tie it up and let it sit in the hot prep kitchen until midnight when our garbage got picked up. We had to get the smell out of the restaurant so the place could air out before our customers arrived, now about two and a half hours away. The garbage can on the corner was also not an option since a smell like this one could incite a riot in our neighborhood.

While Xerxes distributed the fish into small bundles and wrapped them up in fifteen separate bags, I began to shimmy the refrigerator out from against the wall. The plan was for Xerxes to drive around downtown, from Avenue C to Allen Street, and toss small bags of fish into garbage cans about five blocks apart from one another. I was to get the fridge out of the restaurant and into the lot down the street, where we had thrown the first phone booth. While all this was going on, I had three other guys, who looked like bank robbers with napkins tied over their noses, doing prep for the night. By the time Xerxes got in his car and drove away, I realized that there was no way the fridge was going up the stairs. We had brought it down months earlier before the banister was installed on the staircase.

By four o'clock my drill was plugged in and I was loosening the bolts that held the banister in place. My porter, the usual cast of characters from the street, and I struggled to bring the four-hundred-pound fridge up the stairs and down the street to the lot. Xerxes came back at four thirty to oversee the installation of the new fridge while I jumped in his car and raced over to the Chelsea Market, where I bought four hundred dollars' worth of fish at retail prices.

It was five fifteen when I left the fish store. I still had to run back to the Jewelry Exchange to close up quickly before my neighbor, who was watching my booth, left for the night. I also had to get back to the restaurant to fix the banister and get the fish in the new fridge.

I parked on Chrystie Street and bolted to the Jewelry Exchange. From the front door of the building I could see my booth and an animated Gina talking my neighbor's ear off. Gina, a menacing woman from Staten Island and one of my biggest nightmare customers, was the last person I wanted to deal with that day. She had driven to the city with her sweet, mild-mannered fiancé, Angelo, who had spent the last six months searching for the perfect diamond for her engagement ring. Apparently he had popped the question because the ring, a two-carat marquise set in yellow gold, now sat on her pudgy, French-manicured finger.

Her shriek "Jaaaawn!" hit me before I reached my counter, stirring within me the same reaction as the first whiff of rotten fish. "Wheah have you been? I've been waiting heah for twenty minutes."

"Hey, John, how ya doin'?" was all I got from an embarrassed Angelo.

"Jawn, I hate this mounting," she said as she shoved the ring in my face. "It's too low."

"Okay, I can fix it. Why don't you leave it here and I'll reset it," I said.

"I want it to look biggah. I want it high, and I want it fat."

While she was complaining, all I could think about was that in twenty minutes, two parties of six and three parties of four would be sitting down in my restaurant, tasting the fresh ricotta and *filone* bread the waiter would bring to the table. They would see the glow of the oven reflecting in the mirrors in the dining room. Maybe they would try the new white wine I ordered from Sardinia.

I showed Gina my highest and tackiest six-prong setting, promised her that her diamond would look big and fat ("like the roll of fat that's coming out of your too-short shirt," I wanted to say), locked up my merchandise, and left the Jewelry Exchange. As I walked to the car on Chrystie Street, I called Pam and said, "I'm quitting the jewelry business." Her answer was the same as when I asked her to marry me: "Okay."

I reached the spot where I had parked Xerxes' car, a now empty patch of tar and concrete that held a small sign, which read "Tow Away Zone." The car was gone . . . and so was the fish.

Two

FINDING THE SPOT
& DEMOLITION

Back in 2001, when I first started looking for a spot for Ápizz, I got my first taste of how real estate brokers work—and it wasn't pretty. Brokers were telling me I needed to be more flexible and that there was no way I was going to find what I was looking for. But I was very sure about a few things, and I wouldn't bend: I wanted to be on the Lower East Side; I wanted to be off the beaten path, not wedged between a nail salon and dry cleaners, a destination that people would seek out; and I decided it was too risky to pay more than five thousand a month. So, with all this in mind, I spent every morning for six months walking the streets of the Lower East Side, looking for vacant storefronts. Every night, I searched the fifteen New York City real estate websites bookmarked on my computer, only to find properties that I had already seen.

I knew the streets so well that eventually I could recall the smallest details about every location in the neighborhood. When a broker told me about a place three doors in from the corner of Norfolk and Stanton, I would say, "The place with the blue door?" When I heard about a place available on Rivington, I knew immediately that it was the abandoned bakery with the torn red awning.

I saw a lot of crap. There was the "spacious and charming" spot on Clinton that turned out to be a cubbyhole too small for a take-out sandwich shop. Another location that a broker promised was perfect for a restaurant turned out to be on the second floor of a building, right down the hall from a suspicious-looking massage parlor. I could just see New York diners climbing a flight of stairs to eat dinner while listening to the lovely moaning sounds coming through the thin walls. Besides, panna cotta was the only happy ending I wanted on my block. I saw one place with "lots of character" that turned out to be a white-walled, low-ceiling medical office below street level. One night, I was lying in bed when a broker I was dealing with called me at home. I was excited; he must have found something good if he was calling me so late, I thought.

"What do you have for me?" I said when I picked up the phone.

"Hey, can you do me a favor? I need a reservation at Peasant for six people tomorrow night and they're completely booked. Can you get me in?"

Finally, after six months of this, I found something I liked. It was an old vintage comic book gallery on Attorney Street that I had walked by a million times, and it was now empty. I called the number on the large, glossy FOR RENT sign in the window and left a message for the broker handling the property. The company listed on the sign was a big uptown firm, exactly the kind of agency I didn't want to deal with—too corporate for me. Two days later I got a call back from Adam, an aggressive and overly enthusiastic kid.

"What's the square footage on the Attorney Street spot?" I asked

"It's about twenty-two hundred square feet on the main floor and fifteen hundred in the basement," he said.

"What's the build-out?"

"The owner will probably give you three or four months," he said. So far, so good, I thought. Not having to pay rent for four months while I built the place would really help. Now, for the make-or-break question:

"How much?" I asked.

"He wants fifty-five hundred a month, but I'm sure we can get it for forty-five hundred." I thought this was a bit high considering Attorney Street was not well known and completely off the beaten path. But I still thought I could work with all this. During the negotiating process, the numbers usually drop; they don't go up. If fifty-five hundred was my starting point, it wasn't so bad. I thought this scenario could probably only get better.

"When can I see it?" I asked.

"First I'll send you a brochure of our properties, and then we can set up an appointment for you to come to my office." Here we go with the corporate shit, I thought. I knew this brochure would be completely useless to me.

"Let's skip that and just see the spot," I said.

"Uh, well, I probably have a lot of other properties that I can show you. We can schedule a couple back to back."

"I just want to see this one," I said.

"But I have the most perfect three-thousand-square-foot space in Chelsea that you should see," he said.

"Adam, do me a favor and stop selling me. I don't want to hear about anything except what I ask you for. You don't know me, so don't try to sell me on things I'm not interested in." While I had probably said those exact words to nine out of ten brokers I was meeting with at the time, I usually didn't say it within the first minute of the conversation. It seemed Adam was exceptionally gifted at getting under my skin. We set up a time to meet the next day.

You don't see a lot of suits on the Lower East Side, especially in the daytime. So when a nerdy guy in his mid-thirties showed up on Attorney Street wearing a suit and tie, I knew right away it was Adam. He was everything I thought he would be, and so was the space. It had high ceilings, exposed brick, wide wooden plank floors; it was beautiful, except there was no way it was twenty-two hundred square feet. I thought it was more like eighteen hundred square feet and hoped that would help me negotiate a better price.

Since the first day I had started sketching a plan for the restaurant, I envisioned one large brick oven as the main cooking implement and the focal point of the dining room. I thought it would add drama, and with cooks standing in front of it, the oven could be the backdrop of a sort of show for diners. This spot was perfect. I could see where the oven would go, leaving me more than enough room for a fifty-five to sixty seat dining room. Suddenly, I was in the zone, configuring the dining room, waiters' station, and bar in my head, when Adam started giving me the hard sell.

"You can put a bar right over here along this wall," he said pointing to the place where my oven would have to go. "The dining room could start over here by the front door."

"Yeah," I said, "that's perfect if you want your customers to be blasted with cold wind every time the door opens." I knew the dining room would have to start much farther back, and I had already considered the fact that I might have to move the front door in order to make the entrance handicap accessible.

"You should definitely build a mezzanine so you can fit more . . ."

"Adam, have you ever built a restaurant before?" I asked.

"Uh, no."

"Then stop talking."

"Okay, I just want you to . . ."

"Adam, shut up."

I left him on Attorney Street, went home, and started doing numbers, working with a safe middle-ground scenario—an average price of $35 per head and a 50-seat dining room. I figured I would be open for dinner only (there wasn't enough foot traffic on Attorney Street for lunch service), six nights a week (I would have the same staff every night and needed to give them a night off). That gave me 24 business days a month. I divided the rent, $5,500, by 24 and got $229. In addition to this daily rental expense, I estimated it would cost me another $650 per day for expenses like payroll, electricity, garbage pickup, linens, and so on. I added $650 and $229 and got $879, which I rounded up to $900. If I had to make $900 a day just to stay open, I had to figure out the minimum number of people I needed to serve a night. I got this number by dividing $900 by $35, my estimated price per head, and got 25. I needed 25 customers a night just to get by. This felt like a doable number. I called Adam.

"I'll take it," I said.

"Great," he answered. "I'll call the owner."

I began sketching my new restaurant. As I drew, I could really see the dining room take shape around the oven. I could feel the energy of the place. I sketched the exterior and, for the first time, wrote the word *Ápizz* in simple block letters across the top of the storefront. *Ápizz* (ah-BEETS) was the word that my family always used for "pizza" when I was growing up. It was an Italian slang word that you heard a lot in my neighborhood. I was getting excited.

Thirty minutes later, the phone rang. It was Adam.

"Hi, John," he said. I knew right away something was wrong because the usual perky, kiss-ass tone in his voice was gone. "There is a little mistake in the price of the property. I've been going over it and . . ."

"Get to the point," I said.

"It's actually ten thousand a month instead of fifty-five hundred," he said.

"What?"

"When I heard the number *fifty-five,* I thought that meant the rent was fifty-five hundred a month. But what it really meant was fifty-five dollars a square foot."

Ápizz's original exterior: a sweatshop's beauty is in the eye of the beholder

I was fuming. "This is what you do for a living; how could you make that mistake?" I said.

"I don't know how . . ." I hung up the phone. Adam's excuses and apologies would only make me angrier. The bottom line was that I couldn't afford the rent. I called the owner of the building directly and explained the situation, hoping maybe he would say something that would make all this go away. Instead he said to me, "Let's face it, brokers suck."

A few days later, still recovering like a schoolboy getting over a crush, I hit the streets of the Lower East Side once again. This time instead of going straight on Rivington Street like I usually did, I made a left on Eldridge. I wasn't sure why; the strip of Eldridge Street I turned onto was almost completely residential—lots of housing projects sandwiched between two bodegas, one on each corner. But then I saw it, a small one-story, dilapidated building covered with graffiti. There was a small piece of paper taped to the door with a hand-written note, which said "For Rent, See Owner." I was in love.

The restaurant before renovations

I walked across the street to take it all in. There was a large window made up of those cheesy glass bricks that were used a lot in the eighties. I knew immediately that I would get rid of them and cement the wall so my customers wouldn't mix with the gang members on the corner. Above and below the window were rows of old brick; it looked like it was built in the early 1900s, which meant the interior could be pretty cool. The place was totally rundown, but to me, it was a diamond in the rough. I imagined three trees, uplit and spaced evenly in front, and an *Ápizz* sign hanging outside the building at a right angle, so it was visible down the block.

I grabbed the pen from behind my ear, scribbled the number down, and tried not to think about how much I liked this spot. I felt as if I was recovering from the Attorney Street disaster. Just like relationships—getting the new girl's phone number is the first step in forgetting the old one.

Two days later, I was standing on Eldridge Street with Pam waiting for the owner to show us the space.

"Remember," I said, "whether you like it or not, don't show it. Poker face." She nodded with a serious stare as if she were rehearsing. The owner, a local hippie artist who had been part of the neighborhood for the past twenty-five years, came around the corner and showed us in.

The first thing I noticed were these weird, loftlike levels that were supposedly sleeping quarters for former sweatshop workers. Their bulky structures made it hard to see the space as a whole, but once I got past them and walked toward the back of the space, which was empty, the whole room opened up. Pam and I looked around at what seemed to be a beautiful old space covered with new and, in my eyes, ugly drywall and white tiles. The most amazing part was right above us. The ceiling, the only thing that wasn't hidden beneath a blanket of newness, was a mass of old wooden beams and metal brackets that gave way to two skylights. It was stunning. I turned toward Pam, who may as well have been wearing a shirt that said "We'll take it!" She was grinning from ear to ear and both of her thumbs were up. I even caught her jumping up and down once when she thought the owner wasn't looking. "Way to play it cool," I whispered.

I turned to the owner. "How much?"

"Three thousand."

Though the space was a lot smaller than the Attorney Street spot, about 800 square feet on the main floor and only 200 in the basement, where my prep kitchen would have to go, $3,000 a month was very workable. In fact, it was a no-brainer. I held a piece of paper against the wall and jotted down numbers. Once again, I used 24 business days a month and an average price of $35 per head. I divided the rent, $3,000, by 24 and got $125. I added $650 (for additional per-day expenses) to $125 and got $775, which I rounded up to $800. I divided $800 by $35 and saw that I had to serve 23 people a night just to get by. So far, so good, I thought.

I imagined the room with the oven, dining area, and everything else that was needed. I wanted to fit at least 40 to 45 people in the dining room, but I knew there was no way I could do that and also have a bar big enough for people to sit at. I would only have room for a small service bar where waiters could pick up drinks for tables. That meant if a customer's table wasn't ready, he or she would have to wait outside on Eldridge Street. If only the basement was bigger, I thought. If I could somehow dig out more square footage downstairs so that it was equal in size to the main floor, I could fit a prep kitchen, bathroom, and a lounge where people could wait for tables. With no room for people to wait, I didn't see how I could make this work.

"Do you think I could excavate the basement?" I asked the owner.

"It would probably cost you more than a year's worth of rent," he said, "but if you get an engineer to say it's okay, knock yourself out."

"What's the build-out?" I asked.

"I'll give you three months."

"How long a lease can I get?"

"Fifteen years," he said.

"What kind of rent increases are you thinking?" I asked. If this guy saw a lot of potential in the neighborhood and planned on raising the rent by 10 percent each year, this point could easily be a deal breaker.

"Two percent," he said.

"I'll take it."

I heard Pam say "Yesss!" under her breath.

THE DEMOLITION: "WAKE UP, YOU'RE FIRED"

AS SOON AS I got the keys to my new place on Eldridge Street, I walked inside, picked up a sledgehammer, and made a large hole in the wall. The impact sent drywall flying in every direction. I shattered and pulled at jagged pieces for about ten minutes before I finally hit pay dirt—old, beautiful brick. I was so excited that I would be able to reveal a full wall of it; figuring out a way to make the ugly white walls look cool had been nagging at me all week. At the same time, I knew that getting to it meant time-consuming and probably costly demolition. I couldn't afford to waste more than a week of my three-month build-out on simply getting the space raw. I needed to get moving.

There was a loud and relentless banging at the front door. I was expecting Bob, the contractor recommended to me by a friend at the Jewelry Exchange, but the guy standing in front of me was short, huge, and Chinese, not at all a "Bob." He just stood there smiling at me.

"Can I help you?" I asked.

"I'm Bob."

I was caught off guard. I'm not sure what I was expecting, but I definitely didn't envision a three-hundred-pound Buddha. I invited him in.

Bob knocked on a few walls and surveyed the place for about a minute before he spoke.

"You rented this place?" he said with a look of disbelief.

I was used to dealing with people who didn't share my vision. My parents hated the name Peasant, for example. "Why don't you call it 'Johnny's Place'?" they suggested. I knew not to waste time trying to explain my way of thinking to Bob.

The drywall is my drawing board as I sketch plans for the dining room.

The old, beautiful brick hidden behind drywall

"The first thing I need to do is really see what I'm working with here," I said. "I want the paint on the ceiling stripped, the drywall pulled off of every inch of wall space, the tiles picked up, and these lofts removed."

Bob looked down at the large, shiny linoleum, "This tile is nice; you should keep it."

"I want everything out of here," I repeated, "including those glass bricks in the window."

"No problem," he said. "I can do that."

Bob estimated that with three other workers, he could have the job done in one week.

"How much?" I asked. I had heard this guy did decent work and was dirt cheap.

"Four thousand, including carting all the debris away," he said. I hired him on the spot.

The next day Bob arrived with the oddest crew of workers I had ever seen. Angel was a skinny Spanish kid no more than eighteen years old with a bandana tied around his head and lots of religious icons tattooed on his arms; Lim was a toothless, frail, and ancient-looking

Chinese guy with a humpback; and Ray, a stocky, forty-something Polish guy with gin blossoms on his nose, seemed to be drunk at eleven A.M.

I was concerned but thought, this is just demolition. How badly could they mess it up? Bob assigned each guy a job, and they got right to work. Within minutes they were banging, pulling, and prodding at the place, and loosening the screws to dismantle the lofts. Bob was hammering into drywall when I realized he didn't have the keys to the pull-down gate to let himself in.

"Hey Bob," I yelled over the noise. "I'm going to the store to make you a copy of the keys." He stopped hammering and stood there motionless, with his head down. I looked at the floor to see what he was staring at but didn't see anything. "Bob," I shouted again. I inched closer to him and saw that his eyes were closed. I wondered what was wrong with him. I shook his shoulder and said his name again. Suddenly, his eyes opened and he looked right at me and smiled.

"You okay?" I asked.

"Yeah. What's up?" he said, as if everything were perfectly normal.

"I think you kind of zoned out there for a minute."

"Nope, I'm fine," he said.

I left to go to the hardware store with a bad feeling growing inside me. Thirty minutes later, when I got back, Bob's motley crew was making progress. One of the lofts was now a pile of rubble on the floor and the second one was on its way down. Bob was up on a ladder using a crowbar to pull apart the drywall.

I stood there, taking it all in and trying to get a sense of the layout when suddenly, something crashed loudly on the floor a few inches away from me. It was Bob's crowbar. I looked up to see that he was still standing on the ladder several feet above me. His head was down again and his eyes were closed, his short fat body wobbling a bit, threatening to topple down any minute. I looked at the other guys, who looked at each other nervously.

"He's got that disease," whispered Angel. "It's something like necrolepsy. No, no, it's necrophilia."

Since Bob was fast asleep in the middle of all the chaos, I ruled out the possibility he was having sex with dead people. "He's narcoleptic?" I said.

"Yeah, that's it," said Angel, looking up at his boss on the ladder. "Don't worry, he never falls. He'll wake up in a minute and get back to work."

I stared at Angel, in shock at everything that was happening. That's when I caught Ray taking a swig from a flask. Okay, that's it, I thought, this has to be a joke. I looked around for the hidden cameras. There was no way this crew could be for real. I went outside to call the guy at the Jewelry Exchange who had recommended Bob. He basically told me that if I just left him alone, the job would get done. "It's a little sleep disorder; what's the big deal? It won't get in the way of him doing good work," he assured me.

My head was spinning. I had to fire Bob on his first day of work. I couldn't risk him killing me by dropping something on my head. I wondered how long it would take me to replace him, and what kind of delay that would put on my build-out. I was about to go back inside and fire Bob, when he came out to smoke a cigarette.

"You know, boss, we're willing to work through the night," he said. "We could finish the job in half the time."

Was this Bob's MO—dangle a better offer just when he suspected he was going to be let go? In any case, it was working. If I could get the demo done in a few days, I could start building the restaurant before the end of the week.

"You and your guys don't mind working through the night?" I asked.

"Nah, we never sleep."

He's funny too, I thought.

"You get a liquor license yet?" he asked.

"No, but I'm working on it."

"You know, I own a bar in the East Village," he said.

"Oh yeah."

"But I couldn't put the liquor license in my name cause I did time."

"For what?" I asked, imagining him falling asleep in the middle of a robbery.

"Murder," he said matter-of-factly. Bob was full of surprises. "It was self-defense, really," he added. "This guy started a fight with me on the slopes, and I hit him with my ski pole."

The fact that Bob skied shocked me more than anything else—the murder, the sleep disorder, his size, everything. No matter how hard I tried, I couldn't imagine this Buddha swooshing down the slopes. He didn't have an agile bone in his big, round body.

"Well I guess we should get back to work," I said. "Bob? Bob?"

He was sound asleep, leaning against the building, his cigarette dangling from his lips. I woke him up and fired him. I set off to find another crew.

I always say that everything is one phone call away. If you contact the right person when you're looking for something—concert tickets to a sold-out show, free digital cable, get-out-of-jury-duty-free card—you can usually find it on the first call. That was the case with Quang, my new contractor.

A friend of mine who owned a bar in the neighborhood swore that while his English was terrible, Quang's work was outstanding. I had seen the bar top he had built for my friend, it was a beautiful and intricately carved two-inch piece of cherry wood. I set up a time to meet with him the next afternoon.

Quang was a short little Chinese guy with spiky hair, dirty fingernails, and calloused hands, real worker's hands. A good sign, I thought. I walked him through the place and showed him all the demolition that still needed to be done.

"Can you do this?" I asked. He looked at me with a blank stare. I spoke louder, almost shouting. "You do this." I pointed to the rubble, and as if I was playing a game of charades, I mimed that it had to be taken out of the restaurant. He nodded in recognition. "When can you start?" I said.

He laughed. "Tulee days."

"What?"

"Tulee, tulee days." I had no idea what he was saying. "Tulee," he yelled, holding up three fingers.

"Oh, three days," I said. "Sounds good." I rubbed my fingers together, the universal sign for money.

"Two-seven-hundred," he said.

If he meant twenty-seven hundred, it was a great price. I gave Quang a piece of paper and a pen, "How much?" I asked, "You write." He wrote down $2,700. I nodded. I liked this guy already; he was coming in a lot lower than Bob. "When you finish, you build more," I said.

He laughed again, which I took as a "yes."

I didn't know it at the time but Quang would become one of my most valuable guys. He would custom build everything in the restaurant for me, each piece revealing his amazing craftsmanship and attention to detail. He would take slabs of wood and carve out beautiful tables, banquettes, even pizza boards for me, all for a fraction of the cost a typical carpenter would charge. We would learn to communicate using an often hilarious combination of mime and broken English. And when I later put him to work with Paul, the cheap metal guy I found on Chrystie Street, the two made beautiful things together.

Tulee days after I first met Quang, the space was completely empty and raw. I could finally focus on the layout. The first thing I did was pretend I was a customer walking through the front door, which at the time was off on the far right side. I always hated eating at restaurants where the only thing that separated the dining room from the street was a small, semicircular curtained area that surrounded the front door. You see them a lot in small restaurants like mine, where every inch is needed for tables. The problem is, they're never effective. They do nothing to keep out the outdoor elements, and you're basically standing at a hostess stand in the dining room the second you pass through the small entryway.

From the moment I saw the spot from the outside, I loved the idea of creating a secret hideaway on Eldridge, a place that was completely unassuming from the street, but took you by surprise once you walked in. I thought a curtain or cheap plastic divider would instantly kill that feeling of discovery. I needed a vestibule. Not just some small square or rectangular vestibule; I needed a long, narrow one that led people, like a hidden passage, from the front door to a hostess stand several feet inside the restaurant. Not until they were past the hostess would they see the oven and dining room. It would have a great impact. The passageway would also completely block the people sitting at tables from the outside world. I grabbed a roll of black tape and started outlining a long line on the floor to mark where it would go. It was obvious that I could easily fit an additional eight to ten people in the dining room without the vestibule, a precious number when your space is so small. But I didn't care; I thought the privacy it would add would be the difference between an average dining experience and a great one.

In my mind, besides the food, the oven at Ápizz was going to be the most interesting element of the restaurant, one of the main things we would be known for. If it was going to produce every dish on the menu—an idea that, at the time, I thought was very cool but would later come to realize was incredibly challenging—it had to be large and dramatic, a central design element. I'm not talking about a wimpy little dome-shaped oven with a cute little mouth. The oven I was sketching was mammoth, a 10-foot-tall, 11-foot-wide, 6-foot-deep monster of an oven with a mouth large enough to reveal giant, roaring flames. When Quang walked in and saw the black tape on the floor outlining where the oven would go, he said, "Ah, your kitchen go here, no?"

"No," I said. I showed him my drawing, which he stared at for a few minutes before it made sense. Then he started laughing. "Ha, ha, you crazy," he said.

Before I had Quang start working on the vestibule and dining room, I wanted to find out about excavating the basement. A longtime jewelry customer who owned a big Manhattan-based construction company put me in touch with a guy named Steve who ran a midtown firm that specialized in excavation. I had seen the firm's sign on scaffolding around the city for years, which scared me right off the bat. Too big and too expensive for my little job, I thought. It would be like hiring Philippe Starck to build a tree house. Still, I kept my meeting with Steve just to see how it would play out. He came down to meet me at Ápizz wearing a suit and a hard hat. He had a clipboard in one hand and a briefcase in the other. Quang and I were covered from head to toe in dirt and plaster dust.

"It shouldn't be a huge job," I said. "Just a 15-by-15-foot hole."

Steve studied the blueprints of the building that were filed with the city when the place was first built. "Well, the building is certainly sound and can support the work involved," he said. "I'll need a backhoe to dig, and we'll have to remove most of the storefront to gain access."

Ápizz, raw and empty—and about to take shape

"How much?" I said.

"We're talking about a sixty- to seventy-five-thousand-dollar job," he said. "I only work with union help."

My entire budget for building the place would be about $250,000 to $300,000—it was all I had in the bank, and it made sense considering what I spent on Peasant, a much larger restaurant. Steve's price was out of the question, especially since I was only adding 300 square feet. It felt wrong. It was just a hole, I kept thinking. I told Steve to be sure to stop by for dinner once we were open.

My next call was to a friend from Canarsie who owned a carting company and knew a

The crew and I take a lunch break: "Pizza," one of the few words we all understood.

lot of people. He sent over Vincent, a big, scruffy guy wearing a tank top tucked into tight jeans.

"You're a friend of a friend so I'm gonna give you a good deal," he said. Right away, I knew I was in trouble. If Vincent had to say he was going to give me a good deal, he probably wasn't. "I can do it for forty-five thousand," he said.

While it was better than $60,000 to $75,000, $45,000 seemed like a lot for a job that, in my eyes, was time-consuming but was basically just digging. I told Vincent I would think about it.

"I make hole," Quang said suddenly.

"Yeah?"

"I engineer. In China, I work as engineer."

He grabbed my piece of paper from my hand, flipped it over, and started drawing the basement. He sketched support beams and reinforcements, footings, and the foundation beneath the building. Only trained engineers or architects drew those kinds of details. It never occurred to me that he could do the job.

I rubbed my fingers together.

"Maybe tulee-zero thousand."

"Thirty thousand?" I asked.

He nodded.

"Are you sure?" I asked. "Have you done this before?"

"Yeah, no problem. I dig and lay new cement and new walls."

Quang's price was doable. "Okay," I said, knowing I was taking a chance. Something about him felt right.

The next day, Quang showed up with six Mexicans, each one armed with a shovel and pair of gloves, and got to work. Every morning he would go to Roosevelt Avenue in Queens, where day workers would wait on a corner for possible jobs, and pick up six men. Sometimes he would show up with the same guys and sometimes he would bring new ones. It was anyone's guess. Within minutes, Quang and his men broke through the brick and hit dirt. They did by hand what Steve from the big, expensive midtown firm would have done with a backhoe: they dug. They dug into the earth from eight A.M. to seven P.M. stopping once a day for a forty-five-minute lunch break. The bigger the hole got, the more the air turned dank from the soil being unearthed. The space felt like a cave.

One day, we unexpectedly found beautiful old brick in the ground. It was in the shape of a dome. Quang said it was the top of an old building. I had been scouring construction sites looking for brick just like these to put on the face of the oven, which would be built in the next few weeks. But everything I was finding looked so perfect and new and would have made the oven look fake, like a prop. I felt like we stumbled upon gold. Quang just laughed at me as I grabbed them from the buckets and set them aside. "Better you go buy new," he said. "Home Depot, five-zero cents a brick."

At the end of the first week, they started hauling the dirt out of the restaurant and into Quang's van with a very efficient bucket brigade. Three weeks after they began, my basement had grown from 200 square feet to about 500—enough room for a lounge, bathroom, and prep kitchen—and it had new cement walls and a ceiling. Quang had even put in three support I-beams to reinforce the weight of the oven that would be built above. With 300 extra square feet downstairs and a clear image of where everything would go upstairs, I was ready to start building the restaurant.

Three

THE BUILD-OUT

By THE TIME I signed the lease on my new restaurant, my head was spinning from all the "you'll needs" I was hearing from everyone about a liquor license: "You'll need a lot of money," "You'll need to suck up to the Community Board," "You'll need an insider at the State Liquor Authority." It seemed that everyone had someone I needed to talk to, some valuable contact who could facilitate my liquor license quickly and cheaply. And everyone had a horror story of a friend of a friend who spent thirty-five thousand dollars trying to get a license, only to be turned down by the SLA right before they opened.

Someone I knew in the restaurant industry swore to me that his friend Steve, an expediter at the Buildings Department, had all the right contacts and could push my paperwork through with the SLA right away. It was implied that this guy took some shortcuts and might not be altogether legitimate, but my contact urged, "Don't go to a lawyer. I'm telling you, use this guy, and you'll get your license."

"Great," I said. "Give him my number."

Steve called the next day and asked me to meet him on the corner of Second Avenue and Sixth Street. He was a clean-cut guy in his forties who sounded more like a Midwesterner than a New Yorker.

"So, what's the first thing we have to do?" I asked.

"I'm going to take care of everything. Don't worry."

I started to worry.

"I'll need two hundred dollars to get started," he said.

Steve must have sensed that I had a bad feeling about the whole thing because he added, "It's for filing fees and whatnot. I've done this a million times. Don't worry, you'll get your license."

It was only two hundred, I thought. I would take a shot. I reluctantly took the cash out of my pocket, handed it over to Steve, and hoped for the best.

I called him regularly over the next few weeks, asking for updates. "Everything is fine," he always said. "We're moving along." Having never done this before, I didn't have any idea what was supposed to happen. I felt like I had to trust Steve a little while longer. Six weeks after our first meeting, I called him up and insisted we get together again. I wanted to see him face-to-face and find out what kind of progress he was making. We met on the same corner of Sixth Street and Second Avenue.

"It's already been six weeks, how much longer until I get my license?" I asked.

"Just a few more weeks," he said. "But I'll need another two hundred dollars."

"Excuse me?"

"You know how it goes; there are more filing fees and whatnot."

I thought Steve was filing an awful lot of papers and wondered why I hadn't filled out any forms yet. I decided to put an end to this right then and there. I would rather pay more to do this legitimately, I thought, and sleep better at night.

"I'm not giving you another cent," I said.

"I can't do it without more money."

"You can't do it with the money," I said. "We're done. I don't want to hear from you again."

After he walked away, I stood on the street alone, angry at myself for dealing with this guy and anxious about how I was going to get a liquor license in time for my opening. I took a deep breath and looked around. I counted five restaurants that all had liquor licenses on two blocks of Second Avenue alone. Something told me that the owners of all these places were not brilliant, and if they could figure it out, so could I.

The next morning, I read an article in the *New York Times* about how difficult it was getting for New York City nightclub owners to get liquor licenses. The article included a lot of quotes by a guy named Warren Pesetsky, a Manhattan-based lawyer. I thought, this is a guy who gets liquor licenses for people; this guy's an expert. I called him that same day and made an appointment to meet with him. Over the phone, Warren asked me one question. "Just give me the address of your restaurant," he said. I gave it to him and told him I would see him the following week.

I liked Warren right away; he was a straight shooter, plus he represented a long list of impressive restaurants and bars in the city. As soon as I sat down in his office, he told me that my liquor license was feasible. He knew exactly how many liquor licenses were issued on my block and, based on my lot number, knew there were no churches or schools within two hundred feet of Ápizz, a big no-no with the SLA. He also told me I would have to go before Community Board Three and that he had good dealings with them in the past.

"Now, on to some equally important matters," he said. "Do you have a clean record?"

"No felonies if that's what you mean."

"Good. How late will you stay open?"

"Until eleven P.M.," I said.

"Very good. Any outdoor seating?"

"No."

"Perfect."

"How many days a week will you be open?" he asked.

"Six."

"How big will your bar be?"

"No bar stools; just a small service bar," I said.

"Okay, it's a slam dunk," he said.

"I want to open in about three and a half months."

"I think you'll be fine."

When someone was as confident as Warren, I usually felt extremely reluctant, but with him, I had a good feeling right from the start.

"How much will this cost?" I asked, waiting for the thirty-five-thousand-dollar ball to drop.

"Somewhere between forty-five hundred and fifty-five hundred."

"Done," I said.

Less than three months later, I had my license.

All and all, I got off easy. I spent two hundred dollars on an idiot scam artist and five thousand dollars on a legitimate lawyer who knew what he was doing and had a great track record. With all the stories, warnings, and pieces of advice that go around on the dreaded topic of liquor licenses, here's what I think: If you are opening a restaurant in New York, you need to do one thing to get a license—call Warren Pesetsky. And do that *before* you sign your lease.

The Design Team: A Mobster, a Muralist, and a Mouth

When the design process began, I was sure about what I did *not* want. I wasn't interested in anything that resembled an ultra-trendy, highly designed restaurant. No sleek, glossy Plexiglas walls uplit with blue lights for my place. In my mind, restaurants that seem like they're trying way too hard to be trendy are bound to be dated and tired within a year or two. I wanted something that was modern but a bit more timeless (though not traditional), a room that would be as beautiful in ten years as it was new.

I already knew where everything would go: the vestibule would jut straight out from the front door; the hostess stand would be at the end of the vestibule; the service bar would start a few feet behind the hostess stand; the waiters' station, which was where the staff would make coffee, would go against the back wall hidden behind the service bar; and the dishwashing and bussing stations would go on the same back wall, behind the oven. Every other inch of space would be devoted to the dining room. Now I had to figure out the design of each element—curves versus right angles, ornate versus clean lines, color, and materials—and whether or not I should buy them from a restaurant supplier or have them built.

The only thing in the room that had to look really old and rustic was the oven. It was going to be built by a guy named Marshall who had built many wood-burning ovens in New York City restaurants. But they were all small and dome shaped, exactly what I didn't want. I showed Marshall a detailed sketch of what I wanted the oven to look like, including its dimensions.

"This might be the biggest oven in any restaurant in New York," he said after reviewing my drawing. "You sure you want it this big? It's going to take up about fifteen to twenty percent of the whole room."

"I'm sure," I said, thinking that if we ever had to go the desperate, cheesy marketing route, we could run ads that said, "Eat at Ápizz, Home of New York's Largest Wood-Burning Oven!"

"It's too big," he said. "You're not going to have room for the rest of your kitchen."

"The oven will be my kitchen," I said. Marshall looked at me like I was crazy.

"Okay, fine, but the opening of the oven can't be as large as you want it to be," he said. My drawing called for a six-foot-wide mouth. "Too much heat will escape; you need about a two- to three-foot-wide opening."

I didn't really want to bend on this point because the smaller the mouth, the less fire diners would see. The effect wouldn't be nearly as dramatic. But Marshall was the oven expert, so I met him in the middle at four feet. Marshall and his crew would build the oven entirely from cement and fire brick with iron I-beams to support the structure. It would be my job to finish its face to make it look like it had been there for years. Marshall planned to bring in all his materials the following week and begin work on the oven. I left black tape on the floor outlining its edges just to be sure Quang or I didn't build anything else too close to it.

The next thing I focused on was the counter that would go in front of the oven. This would be another big focal point of the restaurant because it would run the length of the oven—eleven feet—and be the only thing that separated my customers from my cooks. Since the top of the counter would be about four feet high and clearly visible, I wanted it to be a beautiful and functional design element. I imagined it covered with stacked terra-cotta pots and lots of bowls full of colorful fruits and vegetables. And I liked the idea of building it out of materials that contrasted with the oven—modern and polished next to old and rustic. For the base, I chose a simple, natural birch wood that Quang brought by one day. For the top, I wanted a glossy concrete. I asked Quang if he could make it.

"I want you to pour concrete for the top," I said, showing him my drawing.

"Okay, first I pour a mode," he said.

"What?"

"A mode, I make mode from wood. Then put concrete."

Oh, a mold, I thought. "Okay, great."

I still needed to figure out what to do with the vestibule. I was anxious to get that built because it would help shape the perimeter of the dining room. One day I was sitting in the middle of the room staring at the space where the vestibule would go and trying to figure out what it should be made out of, when Carmine, a guy I knew from the neighborhood, walked in.

The hardest and definitely most annoying thing I had to deal with when designing my restaurant were the amateur interior designers like Carmine who crawled out of the woodwork to offer unsolicited opinions. Unfortunately, Carmine was just one of my many unwanted "design consultants." They all thought they knew what a restaurant should look like, but no matter what they said—"a rotating dessert tray would be perfect in here," "the waiters should wear tuxedos," "you need a fountain"—they didn't have a clue about what was right for *my* restaurant. Designing a restaurant is like designing a home: it's personal. I would never walk into Carmine's house and say, "That red velvet painting of the Leaning Tower of Pisa doesn't work with that green plastic-covered couch."

Although he drove a bus for the city and probably never broke a law in his life, Carmine desperately wanted people to think he was a gangster. He thought it was his birthright, having been born in Little Italy. He would take out thick rolls of one-dollar bills, held together with a rubber band, and peel off singles for the bartender at Peasant, trying to copy a move he saw in *Good Fellas.*

"Hey, Johnnie," he said.

"What's up, Carm?"

"I heard you were here and came by to see if you needed anything."

"Nope, I'm fine." I really didn't want to be bothered; I needed to focus on the room.

"You know," he said, "my cousin

The mouth that would roar: the foundation of my oven

Paulie sings a couple nights a week over at Palucci's. He really packs them in. He sings a mirage of Sinatra, Bennett, Louis Prima, all those guys. I can get him to do a night over here if you want."

"That's okay, Carmine. I'm just going to play some CDs for background music," I said, trying to figure out what a mirage of music was.

"Okay. Then I can get you some nice stereo equipment for the place. You know, with a built-in CD player."

"That's okay, Carmine. I got it covered."

Carmine was always trying to pull moves like this, but they were never really illegal. A few weeks earlier, he had come up to me on the Bowery to show me a Rolex he had just "acquired."

"Let's just say it fell off a truck," he said, looking around nervously. My years at the Jewelry Exchange taught me how to spot a fake a mile away, and Carmine's watch was nothing if not fake. The gold was way too shiny.

"This is valuable," I said, playing along. "You better put it away."

"Yeah, you're right; there's a lot of heat on this right now."

Now he was standing in the restaurant disrupting me while I was trying to design the vestibule. I tried to ignore him, hoping he would go away, but as my luck would have it, he was feeling creative and in the mood to dispense some free design advice.

"Johnny," he said, looking at the large boarded-up window in the restaurant, "you know what would be really nice over there? Red curtains."

"I'll think about it."

"It would make the place very classy," he said.

Metal and glass, I thought. It would be interesting to bring some metal and glass into the room through the vestibule.

"You know what else you could do?" he said.

"Uh huh," I mumbled. I couldn't use glass for the entire structure, I thought, because I didn't want people who were walking into the restaurant to be able to see the dining room. I had to use something that was opaque.

Carmine went on, "You could throw some nice red-checkered tablecloths on the tables; they would match the curtains." I had grown up going to the red-checkered Italian *ristorante;* it was something I definitely didn't want to do.

I focused again on the vestibule. What if I used long, thick pieces of wood and lay them horizontally, three-quarters of the way up? I could use glass from the top of the wood all the way up to the ceiling. That would allow light to pass through from the top and make the structure feel less bulky. I could wrap the entire thing in metal for a modern finish. I started sketching, simultaneously devising a plan to get rid of Carmine.

"You should probably get out of here," I finally said. "I'm expecting the captain of the Fifth Precinct any minute. He wants to talk to me about joining some neighborhood organization," I lied, knowing he would take the bait.

"Oh, yeah, I better hit the road. Me and cops, we're like oil and vinegar; you know what I'm saying?" He left, mumbling something about stoolies.

This new design really depended on the right wood. I took out my tape measure and ran it along the black tape on the floor marking off the vestibule. I would need four large pieces of wood, each about 16 feet long and 1½ feet high, stacked one on top of the other to create a wall. I could really see the design and materials in my head, and the more it took shape, the more excited I got. The vein in my right temple, the same one that acted up when I was furious, felt like it was working overtime as my adrenaline pumped. I needed to find the wood right away.

I rented a car and started hitting lumberyards in search of my dream wood for the vestibule. While I was at it, I hoped to find the right piece for the front door. Keeping with my speakeasy theme, I wanted to build a grand, oversized front door out of wood that gave you a sense there was something mysterious and private behind it.

I drove to four lumberyards in Queens on the first day and found only plywood, nothing thicker than one inch. The second day brought more of the same in Brooklyn. One yard in Coney Island had the most beautiful piece of mahogany. I fell in love with its rich orangey-red color, but it was too small. I had to find a bigger version.

"I need that mahogany you got out there, but sixteen feet long," I said to the guy who worked at the lumberyard.

"You're not going to find it," he said. "No one has one piece that big. You're going to have to get two pieces and put them together."

I knew the wood I wanted had to exist; I just had to find it. I left Coney Island and drove back to Ápizz, thinking about which borough to hit next. I decided on the Bronx. I took out the Yellow Pages I had brought from home, sat down on a lowboy refrigerator that needed to be installed downstairs, and began making a list. I was about to leave the restaurant when Barbara, another one of my "design consultants," walked in. Barbara was a fifty-five-year-old mom from New Jersey who had worked part time at the Jewelry Exchange for the past fifteen years. Everything about her was big: glasses, gold jewelry, hair, nails, bag, everything. She even talked big, her mouth opening far and wide with every word. I wished the mouth of my oven could be that big. Barbara liked to impress me with what she referred to as her "lavish lifestyle." She would say things like, "My dining set finally arrived from Italy. It came in three pieces," her mouth really stretching on the word *three*.

"Well, look at you," she said now, checking me out from head to toe. Barbara was used to seeing me at the Jewelry Exchange, where I actually put some thought into what I wore every day. Here I was, standing before her in dirty carpenter's pants and an equally dirty T-shirt. "As I live and breathe," she added dramatically, "I never thought I would see you in anything but pressed pants." She looked around. "So this is it."

"Yeah, Barbara, this is it. I'm actually on my way . . ."

"Did you hire a designer yet?"

"No, I'm doing it myself."

"Oh, that's good," she said unconvincingly.

I kept saying "Leave, leave, leave, leave" over and over again in my head.

"Have you decided on a color scheme?"

A color scheme? I thought. What was I decorating, a bar mitzvah?

"I just redid my living room," she said. "John, it's gor-geous. Not for nothing, but my neighbors are dropping dead over it. They all want me to decorate their houses."

"That's great, Barbara, but I . . ."

"This room is very cold. The right rug would really warm it up, make the place very elegant," she said.

"Barbara, I have to go. I have an appointment uptown. Come on, I'll walk you out."

I didn't hear another word that came out of her big mouth. I walked her to her Cadillac, watched her get in, shut the driver's side door, and walked away. I didn't even wave when she drove by me and honked twice. I had tunnel vision for getting to the Bronx.

My first stop in the Bronx was Rosensweig's Lumber, a seedy-looking yard in Hunt's Point near all the hookers. I didn't bother calling in advance because I had been phoning places all week and kept getting the exact same answer: "Stuff comes and goes every day, you have to take a look through our stock."

I walked into the store and found the only guy there. "You got any mahogany?" I asked.

"Yeah, we should have a few pieces somewhere out back," he said without looking up. He was holding one of those small, battery-powered fans with a plastic propeller up to his face. I walked out of the store and into the yard, completely unaware of how huge it was. There must have been twelve to fifteen aisles of wood stacked on top of each other. I started walking through them, methodically scanning each pile from top to bottom, trying to make sense of what was there. I saw rows and rows of loglike pieces of wood, nothing less than 10 feet in length or thinner than 1½ inches. This wasn't the wood I wanted—it was much darker, more like a walnut color—but I was encouraged because these pieces were huge. I kept going, checking out aisles six, seven, eight, and nine and seeing more of the same. But then I turned onto aisle ten. It looked different. I noticed it as soon as I turned the corner: wood in deep red, orange, and amber tones. It was mahogany. There was a ton of it in every shape and size imaginable. I felt so lucky. I ran back to the store and ordered four pieces for the vestibule and one piece, 8 feet long by 4 feet wide, for the door. It cost $1,200, including next-day delivery.

My big score—the perfect piece of mahogany for the front door

On the drive back to the city, I called Paul, the metal guy I found on Chrystie Street, and arranged to meet him at the restaurant. I wanted to talk to him about finishing the vestibule in metal. I calculated the timing of the build-out in my head: I had already been in the spot for two months, which meant I had one month left before I would have to start paying rent. I guessed that the oven and counter would be finished within another week, and I hoped Paul and Quang could work together immediately on the vestibule. My goal was to start designing the dining room within five to seven days.

When I walked into Ápizz, I was still going over my To Do list in my head, and didn't even notice another one of my "design consultants," Uri, sitting in the middle of the restau-

The much-needed vestibule separates diners from the outside elements.

rant. Uri was the Ukrainian super of the tenement building next door. Next to Carmine, he was the biggest thorn in my side. He dropped in regularly to offer his carpentry and design advice and waited for me to throw something away, so he could take it home. I knew his apartment was filled with everything from the old sewing machines we had thrown out from the former sweatshop to milk crates like the one he was now sitting on. The problem was that Uri was the consultant with the most time to devote to the project; he could stand around for hours without budging.

"Hey, Uri," I said. "I'm a little busy right now; what's up?"

"I come up with great idea for wall over there," he said, pointing to the big brick wall behind me. "A mural." He paused for dramatic effect. "In Ukraine, we have beautiful city skyline. My cousin, he can paint for you."

I couldn't believe how bad his idea was, and it wasn't just the whole mural thing; it was the Ukraine skyline part. "I don't think so, Uri." I said. "I really have to get back to work."

"Okay," he said. But of course, he didn't leave. Instead he pushed down on the milk crate, testing its strength. "This is nice crate."

Just when I thought things couldn't get worse, Carmine walked in.

"Hey, Johnnie," he said loudly.

I mumbled hello. I have to put a stop to this, I thought.

Carmine looked over at Uri and whispered to me, "It's okay to talk in front of him?" as if he was about to share some news about a murder that just went down.

"Huh?" I said.

"You vouch for that guy?"

I gave Carmine the answer I knew he wanted. "Yeah," I said. "Uri's with me; he's good people."

"Yeah, okay." Carmine said. "I have good news. I got a guy who can get you a bunch of those old jugs of Chianti. You could hang them from the ceiling." Carmine didn't know any "guys," I thought. The jugs were probably sitting in his mother's basement.

"No, that's okay," I said.

"Hel-lo?" Barbara said, walking in. "I'm back."

What a lucky day for me, I thought. My whole "design team" is here together.

"John, I forgot that I had these paint brochures in my trunk. They are fab-u-lous. Can you believe I almost drove back to Jersey without showing them to you?"

"Barbara, I can't believe it," I said.

"Now I really love this mauve. What do you think? We could do accents in rose and . . ."

I had to figure out a way to get rid of them. The problem, I realized, was the design team's easy access to the restaurant. The front door to Ápizz was never locked; the lock was busted. I used the roll-down gate to close up at night. I decided to save myself right then and there and made a beeline for the door. I ran to the hardware store and bought a dead bolt. As soon as I got back, I would have Quang drop whatever he was doing and install it. It was the least rude way I could think of to fire my design team once and for all.

I'm Down with OCD

I WAS IN THE MIDDLE of designing Ápizz when Pam dragged me away to have dinner at a downtown restaurant for which she was thinking about doing publicity. I didn't really have time to go—I was up to my eyeballs in the build-out of the vestibule and oven—so I decided to turn it into a sort of market research opportunity.

The restaurant was twice the size of Ápizz with a table setup that was pretty typical of most New York City restaurants, a mixture of standard-size two- and four-tops. Table size and layout was something I was analyzing that night, since I would soon be ready to buy tables for Ápizz. In fact, I had been obsessing over tables so much over the past thirty-six hours that Pam didn't even ask what I was doing when I first took the tape measure out of my pocket. She just looked over her shoulder to make sure the owner, someone she might want to work with, wasn't watching. Then she started to quietly sing a line from the song she had just written for me; "John's down with OCD, yeah you know me . . ." According to Pam and Xerxes, my manager, my slight case of obsessive compulsive disorder had taken on a life of its own since I started designing my restaurant.

After we placed our order and our waitress was out of sight, I began to jot down numbers on a small piece of paper. I tried to be as nonchalant as possible as I measured two sides of our table. It was a twenty-four-inch square, the size of the usual two-top sold on the Bowery. Next I measured the distance between our table and the one next to us, which was occupied by two people.

"John!" Pam warned.

"What? I said excuse me. Do you believe these tables are only three inches apart?" I said.

Pam just shrugged. "It's pretty typical."

It was true, I thought. New Yorkers were so accustomed to small, cramped tables on top of one another that it didn't even faze us anymore. While I didn't have the room for over-sized, well-spaced tables, I hoped to find a nice middle ground at Ápizz.

Seven minutes after we ordered, our appetizers—grilled octopus and a bread salad—were served. I marked the time on my piece of paper, along with the size of the plates, which were eight inches.

"I think our apps came out too quickly, don't you?" I said.

"Yes. It makes you think they were cooked ahead of time," Pam agreed.

On the other hand, I thought, if you waited too long for appetizers, say 18 to 20 minutes, you'd probably be annoyed since it's your first course. I decided somewhere between 12 to 15 minutes would be perfect. I jotted down the numbers.

Seventeen minutes after our apps were cleared, the same runner who brought out the first course came over with our entrées. Before I began to eat, I took an inventory of our table: there were two entrée plates, which measured 12 inches in diameter; two wineglasses; two water glasses; a large bottle of water; a 6 x 4-inch basket of bread; and a 5-inch dish of olive oil. The table was, in my opinion, way too crowded. I could have easily knocked something over just by reaching for my water glass.

"You should know that the bone in my osso buco is about one and a half inches wide and there is approximately half a teaspoon of marrow inside," Pam said. "And, by the way, it's delicious. I think I want to work with them." She looked at my paper, now covered with numbers. "You can write down that it took me thirty-three and a half minutes to make my decision."

"My risotto is good, too," I said. "What do you think of the runner?"

"I don't know; he doesn't seem to have much of a personality."

"No," I said. "What do you think about the idea of a runner bringing out your food?"

"As long as my food is good, I don't care who brings it out," she said.

It occured to me that since the runner brought out our food, we hadn't really spoken to our waitress since we ordered. It made the experience feel less personal. I took out my scrap of paper and wrote, "Waiter brings food, checks back with customer."

Though I had a list of things I would have changed at this restaurant, we had a great meal. I finally put my tape measure away and we got up to leave. On the way out, Pam told the owner she would be happy to work with them, and they set up a meeting for the end of the week.

After dinner I couldn't wait to get back to Ápizz. As soon as Pam and I walked in, I took a piece of cardboard from an empty box and cut it into a 26-inch square, 2 inches bigger than

The finished exterior

the table we just ate on (and all the two-tops I had seen at restaurant supply stores). I placed it on top of a small step ladder. Then I cut two rough circles 10 inches in diameter, 2 inches smaller than the plates we had just eaten from. I grabbed two rolls of masking tape for the wine and water bottles, and an empty Styrofoam coffee cup and can of Diet Coke for water glasses. My tape measure played the part of a votive, and Pam's sandal stood in for the bread basket. We pulled up chairs and sat down at our mock table. There was plenty of room for two more glasses and even our elbows. I cut four more tables in the same size and placed them on top of stacked cans of wood varnish, in a row next to the first one. This looked good, I thought. Twenty-six by twenty-six were my numbers. I got up and paced the room, measuring to see how many tables I could fit along each wall.

"I think I'll have room for seven two-tops along the edge of the room and three four-

A mirrored view of Ápizz

tops down the center aisle," I said. I sat down again and began sketching a table layout for the whole room, trying to figure out how much wood Quang would need to custom build my new two-tops.

My makeshift table was facing the oven, which at the time was still a skeleton. I could imagine sitting there while eating and staring at its flames, a dramatic backdrop for dinner. I realized that Pam, who was opposite me, was staring at a blank wall.

"What do you think about a mirror on that wall?" I asked.

"I think that would be really nice; it would reflect the fire."

"Exactly," I said. I looked at my watch; I had twenty minutes before the hardware store down the street closed.

"Wait here," I said.

Fifteen minutes later, I walked back into the restaurant holding one of those cheap closet-door mirrors. I grabbed the masking tape and started taping it up horizontally to the cement wall, its warped glass throwing twisted images around the room.

"This will give us an idea of what a mirror would be like over here," I said.

Pam just stared at me and said, "It's going to be a long night."

THREE WEEKS LATER, and less than a month before my opening, I stood outside my restaurant on a hot summer night. I loved the front door, a huge and stunning piece of wood with metal trim, which perfectly conveyed that sense of discovery I was after. I pulled it open and walked inside, making my way through the sixteen-foot-long passageway, which was now my vestibule. The long, wide slabs of mahogany, wrapped in metal, blocked off my view of the restaurant and separated me from the space where diners would eventually sit. But the real experience began at the end of the vestibule, where I was smacked in the face by the oven, now finished and lit for the first time. It was a huge work of art that seemed to have been there forever.

I turned and faced the dining room, which was completely set up with Quang's tables, banquettes, and light wood chairs. Eighteen tables, which meant forty-three seats in all. Two adjacent strips of mirrors, which seemed to float off the walls, were backlit, diffusing a subtle glow throughout the room. In front of the oven was the polished concrete counter, over-flowing with bottles of olive oil and bowls of artichokes, red peppers, and tomatoes.

I made my way downstairs. My new lounge was finished, its wood-beamed ceiling carefully lit. Cozy banquettes lined the perimeter of the room, facing tables and small cushioned stools. I had left a small rock wall exposed, which we had uncovered during the excavation. Its rough edges cut a beautiful contrast to the modern lines of the ceiling and furniture. I continued on to the prep kitchen, where a stainless steel cooking island stood in the center under a ton of pots and pans hanging from the ceiling. The perimeter of the kitchen was lined with glass refrigerators, which would soon hold all of our ingredients. I walked back upstairs and dimmed the two overhead lights that hung from the dining room ceiling. The transformation was immediate and dramatic. The room, bathed in the oven's light, seemed to glow. I sat down in the middle of the room and watched the oven's flames jump in the mirror opposite me. I loved the room. I was now ready to hire my staff.

Four

DOWN TO THE WIRE: PREOPENING SCRAMBLE

MY BUILD-OUT PERIOD had come and gone, and my three months of free rent were over. I sat down at the small desk in the prep kitchen and wrote a check to my landlord for three thousand dollars. I was anxious to get the place open; every day that I was not doing business was now costing me money. I was still really busy with the hundreds of details that were creeping up on me—things like getting the lighting just right and installing the HVAC system to cool and heat the room, exhaust for the oven, and sprinkler system—and I didn't have much time to devote to the food and menu. I had one major problem. I, like many restaurateurs, was not a chef. So I hired a consulting chef, a guy named Rudy, who was going to help me find and train my kitchen staff.

Before Rudy could begin to design a menu, he was pushing me to decide on a clear identity for our food. I kept saying "Italian," and he was telling me to be more specific.

"Italian is pretty specific," I said.

"No," he replied, "you need to really hone in. You should pick a city in Italy."

To me, this sounded ridiculous. For the sake of having an identity, I wasn't going to pick some Italian city that would limit me to a specific style of food that I wasn't passionate about to begin with. Since Ápizz was a Neapolitan slang word, I thought about southern Italian food. I knew that many of the dishes I loved and wanted on our menu—mussels and octopus, pork chops with vinegar peppers, fresh fish with capers and olives—fell into this category. I called Rudy and said, "Southern it is."

"How about Sicilian?" he asked.

"Look," I said. "I'm not a chef, but I know what I want: pizzas, lasagna, ravioli, and amazing meatballs. I think southern Italian is specific enough."

"Okay, but . . ."

"I'm sure about this," I said. "I also want fish and meat dishes. There are a lot of beautiful southern fish and meat dishes that will work really well in the oven."

Now that he had an identity, Rudy began to choose dishes for our menu. He created recipes that we both liked, and he seemed good at choosing ingredients that would appeal to the general public. When I suggested an oven-baked *seppiolini* (cuttlefish) appetizer, a real southern Italian specialty, he thought it might be wiser to do it with calamari instead. "People are really comfortable with calamari," he said. "*Seppiolini* might scare them."

Using a wood-burning oven to cook everything was proving more and more challenging. Every once in a while Rudy would call me all excited about the idea of putting something like seafood risotto on the menu. But I would reply, "Doesn't that require a sauté?" reminding him that everything needed to be oven friendly. Even simple pasta dishes like *linguine vongole* (linguine with clams) were out of the question since we didn't have a stove top upstairs.

We came up with a relatively simple menu with lots of Italian comfort food. There would be eight appetizers, including cold and hot seafood dishes like a mixed seafood salad and wood-baked mussels, as well as three pizzas and eight entrées, such as spinach lasagna, ravioli with brown butter and sage, whole fish, eggplant rollatini, and meatballs made with veal, pork, and beef. I always loved homemade meatballs as a kid and thought it was hard to find really good ones in restaurants. Instead of serving them as a side dish next to a plate of pasta, I wanted to make an entrée out of them: two oversized meatballs with ricotta cheese and a simple tomato sauce. That would be something I would order.

With our menu set, all we had to do was find a cooking staff, and we would be in business. The first guys I met were Ian, Lorenzo, and Marco. Rudy had worked with all three at different restaurants and assured me they were talented and really knew their way around a kitchen. "Remember," I said, "our kitchen has one oven and that's it. I'm sure it's different from anything these guys are used to."

If I liked them, Lorenzo and Marco would cook on the line together with Ian, the only

American of the group, who would be head chef. Ian had graduated from the Culinary Institute of America five years earlier and had since worked in four different kitchens around the city: two Italian, one French, and one American. He was in his late twenties and seemed eager to be a star.

"I've been a sous-chef for about two years now," he said, "and I think I'm ready to be at the helm." I didn't know or care about titles. I just wanted to see if he could cook.

"Who's going to be my garde-manger?" he asked.

"What's a garde-manger?"

"It's my cold station; who's going to man my cold station?"

I thought this guy was a bit pretentious, especially since he was an American standing in an Italian restaurant on the Lower East Side talking to someone he knew probably didn't have a clue about French kitchen terms.

"Have you ever worked with a brick oven before?" I asked.

"Oh, yeah," he said. "I have lots of experience with them. I worked at a brick-oven pizza place in Connecticut right after high school."

Next up were Lorenzo and Marco, who were as different from Ian as you could get. While they each had more cooking experience than he, they didn't seem to care at all about titles or creativity. They just wanted to work, and even seemed disappointed when I told them we weren't going to be open for brunch. Lorenzo and Marco had both been prep and line cooks at very respectable Italian restaurants in New York and had no problem doing the tedious stuff like chopping vats of parsley and shallots and rolling out a hundred pizza doughs a night. I liked them both right away. Rudy had warned me that their English was not great—Lorenzo was El Salvadorian and Marco was Ecuadorian—but I wasn't fazed. I had just spent the past four months building an entire restaurant with Quang.

All that was left to do before hiring the three of them was to make sure I liked the way their food tasted. They went downstairs with Rudy, who had arranged for ingredients to be delivered earlier in the day, and started cooking. Lorenzo started chopping onions and garlic for sauce, and Marco mixed together ground veal, pork, and beef with herbs for the meatballs. Ian made pizza dough and prepped eggplant for the rollatini and squid for the herb-breaded calamari appetizer. In the meantime, I lit the wood-burning oven and allowed it to heat up.

About two hours later, they came upstairs, each man holding a tray of stainless steel tins filled with ingredients. They stood side by side between the oven and the counter and assembled their dishes in terra-cotta pots before putting them in the oven. Lorenzo and Marco carefully tended their dishes while Ian, ever the showman, tossed dough high in the air.

I tasted each dish, paying careful attention to flavor, texture, and temperature. Everything was good, but nothing was perfect. The eggplant rollatini was flavorful but a bit watery. The pizzas were too doughy, and there wasn't enough cheese on top. The calamari was too garlicky and chewy. I saved the meatballs for last, partly because they were my favorite and partly because the plate was so hot, the tomato sauce on top was still bubbling. I pierced one with my fork and took a bite. It was ice cold in the center. I tried the meat on the outside, which was clearly well done. It was really flavorful but a bit dense. I was worried.

"You know, John," Rudy said, "It's going to take some time for these guys to get used to the oven. There are a lot of hot and cold spots in there. But once they do, the food will be great." I knew the oven was going to be tricky and that my cooks would only be able to perfect it through trial and error. I wished I had more time to figure it out myself, but from a financial standpoint, I had to open in about a week. This was the one thing I couldn't do myself. I could dig a hole in Manhattan to find more room for a basement, and I could hunt down the perfect piece of mahogany, but unfortunately I just didn't have the time to figure out the nuances of the oven and teach myself to cook. I hired all three guys.

HIRING MY STAFF:
A WAITER TAKES A SHOT

I SET UP A TASTING at Ápizz so our new staff of waiters, bartenders, and busboys could try each dish and be more knowledgeable about our food. I could hear snippets of the usual banter that comes with meeting someone you'll eventually be working with side by side: "That's cool, man, where does your band play?" and "Where did you work before here?"

My manager Xerxes scanned the room and said to me, "Carson is missing." Carson was one of our waiters, and he was ten minutes late, not a good sign on your very first day of work.

"Carson better get here before the first plate hits the table, or he's going to be fired before he even starts working," I said.

The cooks were busy taking sizzling terra-cotta dishes out of the oven and divvying up small portions of each dish on the menu among several dinner plates for everyone to try. I saw Xerxes nervously look at his watch and knew that he was more worried about having to revisit the pile of résumés we had received than about firing Carson.

Within minutes of posting a Help Wanted ad on Craig's List for waiters, busboys, and bartenders, our fax machine was flooded with résumés. It didn't take long to go through them. We quickly scanned them, looking for a key word that would help us decide which pile to put them in. Anything that said Applebees, Friday's, or Olive Garden went in the "no" pile, along with résumés that mentioned experience in corporate cafeterias. I threw one guy's résumé out because he described the last restaurant he had worked at as a "sheik dining establishment." Xerxes got rid of one applicant because in her cover letter, she referred to herself in the third person. He figured he would never get through the interview with a straight face. "So, Michelle, how many years of serving experience does Michelle have?"

In one day we had hired an entire staff of three waiters, who would rotate shifts, and one bartender and busboy, who wanted to work every night. Now they were all here, ready to work, except for Carson.

Lorenzo brought out the first dish, small slices of *pizza margherita,* and placed a small plate in front of each person. I looked over at Xerxes and shook my head. That's when the front door flew open and Carson charged in, hyper and sweating.

"Dude, I just got shot!" he yelled to me.

"What?" I said. I looked him over to see if he was bleeding. "Are you okay, are you bleeding?" I asked.

"No, I think I'm okay. I think it just grazed me."

"Come with me," I said, taking him back outside. I was going to find these guys. Out on the street, I looked around for anyone who could shed some light on what happened.

"I can't believe this," I said. "Where did it graze you?"

Carson looked down and mumbled something I couldn't hear.

"What did you say?"

"I got hit in the ass, man."

"Did you see the bullet?" I asked. "Was it loud?"

"It was more like a snapping sound than anything else," he replied.

I looked over Carson's shoulder, down Eldridge Street, and saw two figures running toward us. I felt my body go into that tense mode that happened when a fight was about to go down. But as they got closer, I saw that they were two small boys, no older than nine. One ran across the street while one hid behind a car parked in front of Ápizz. They were both carrying plastic BB guns. The boy closest to us looked over at Carson and said, "Sorry, mister."

"A BB gun? You got capped with a BB gun?" I wondered if this was an acceptable excuse for being late. I took Carson back inside.

"Go sit down and try some food," I said. "Do you want a cushion for your wound?"

"No, I better stand," he answered in a serious voice.

Months later, a nice family from Arkansas came in for dinner at the restaurant one night. I heard the mother say that she was nervous about coming down to the Lower East Side. Then her little boy asked with wide eyes if there were any gang shootings in the neighborhood. Carson, who turned out to be one of our best waiters, said in a slightly bragging tone, "Actually, I took one in the back." We made fun of him for the rest of the night, and I made sure he never told the story again.

At the tasting, I joined my new staff and sampled every dish on the menu. While they were oohing and aahing over every bite that passed their lips, I was giving the food a cooler appraisal. It was definitely better than it had been a week earlier when I had first met my cooks, but it still wasn't great. I wasn't going to go by what the waiters thought; what else would they say in front of their new boss? We were opening in less than a week, and we still had a long way to go.

PR: THE PRESS WAITS FOR NO MAN

IT DOESN'T TAKE LONG for a Manhattan restaurant owner to realize he needs PR. It is one of the many necessities—like hiring cooks and setting up accounts with food purveyors—that comes along with opening a place in the city. Thank god I was married to my publicist. PR typically costs a restaurant owner three to four thousand dollars a month with a six-month commitment, but for me it was free.

I had first realized how valuable PR was when Frank DeCarlo and I opened Peasant. For weeks before the opening, I worried about whether or not anyone, besides my family, would show up for dinner. Since we weren't placing any ads—that was considered cheesy in New York, a city where word of mouth is everything—I wondered how people would know about us. That's where PR came in. As our publicist, it was Pam's job to make sure that the local papers, magazines, and websites announced our opening. Afterward, when the business that came in from those opening announcements leveled off, she had to keep our name in the news on an ongoing basis so that no one forgot about us.

I knew Pam was going to get us a lot of opening press. I also knew that once we got this kind of press, we would be on restaurant critics' radar screens and could get reviewed at any time. Pam, who had seen other restaurant clients get reviewed before they had all their kinks worked out, kept telling me, "Be ready."

The bad news was that I knew we weren't. Our cooks were working hard to perfect the oven, but they weren't quite there yet. I decided to delay our opening by another week so we could devote a few nights to serving friends and family. Even though this meant I was losing more money, I thought we desperately needed a few test runs before opening to the public.

As I continued to agonize over the food, tables, and lighting, Pam began to obsess over the *New York Times, New York* magazine, and *Time Out New York,* the three media outlets in which new restaurants need to be covered. The fact that we were on a street most people had never heard of made the need even greater.

"We *have* to get in all three," she said over and over again.

"Don't worry so much," I said. "If we do the right thing, serve good food, and have friendly service, they'll get around to noticing us."

"Hel-lo? We're on Eldridge Street," she said with this crazy look in her eyes, probably the same one I wore when I fell into one of my OCD episodes. "We can't wait around for them to notice us. No one is walking by. Swarms of people aren't passing Eldridge Street on their way to the subway every day. If we don't get the word out, we're going to be in trouble." The funny thing was, this crazy-woman-on-a-mission mode that my wife was in reassured me that my restaurant would get the press it needed. People that determined usually don't fail. On the other hand, I wondered if Ápizz would live up to the media attention.

Though our opening was scheduled for early September, Pam had started working on Ápizz's press kit back in July when she first pitched Florence Fabricant, one of the *New York Times*'s food writers. Fabricant wrote a regular column about restaurant openings and closings as well as news about chefs. She mentioned Ápizz's upcoming fall opening in a mid-summer column. In addition to including my name, she mentioned that we were building an oven as "big as a studio apartment." I was on a high from that item. It was only four sentences, but to me it was unbelievably exciting.

As our opening approached, Pam confirmed that Ápizz would be included in *New York* magazine's and *Time Out New York's* fall preview guides, special issues that featured all the new and interesting cultural events and restaurant openings during the coming fall season. Both magazines would include small write-ups on Ápizz along with a photo.

The first photographer to shoot Ápizz was a young guy from *Time Out* with super-low-waisted jeans and wild curly hair. *Time Out* wanted a shot of a plate of food in front of the oven, so I spent fifteen minutes meticulously plating two meatballs in a large terra-cotta pot, each with a bright red dollop of sauce and a perfect basil leaf on top.

"Oooh, that's good, that's good. Can you move your meatballs a little closer? I want to see the steam coming off them." It sounded more like a photo shoot for a porn magazine than for a local entertainment guide. I saw Pam trying not to laugh.

"Oh yeah, that's nice," the photographer said, looking at the LCD screen on the back of his digital camera. "That's the money shot," he said. "I'm done."

I came from a world where cash is king and tipping is mandatory. The kid had gotten the shot and I was excited. I handed him a twenty.

"Hey, thanks a lot for coming in," I said as I gave him the money.

"Uh," he looked around nervously, "I can't take that, but thanks."

Pam came running over to me with a strange look on her face. "Did you just give him money?" she said.

"I tried to, but he wouldn't take it."

"You're not supposed to offer anyone from the media cash. I don't want anyone to think we're trying to buy an item in a magazine."

"He's a young kid, I thought it would be a nice gesture," I said.

"You can grease your expediter but don't grease *Time Out New York,* okay?"

The next day, we repeated the process—without the tipping—with *New York* magazine, which wanted a photo of me in front of the oven. The photographer told us that the item would run the week we opened, one week after *Time Out's* item would appear. This meant two nice pieces of coverage back-to-back. We really needed to be ready, I thought.

First, we had to get through two nights of serving friends and family. We had handed out postcards to about forty people and asked them to call in and reserve a table for one or both nights. In addition to testing out the food and service, I wanted Xerxes to get some practice booking up the room.

A table of six people I had worked with for years at the Jewelry Exchange walked in first, followed immediately by three four-tops of my cousins. It was exciting seeing my dining room filled with people for the first time and feeling the room's energy. Anthony, my cousin who works as a New York City detective during the day and runs his own tattoo shop on Long Island at night, came running over to me before sitting down.

"This place is sweet," he said, giving me a huge hug. "Hey, check this out." He extended his forearm in front of me and turned it over so I could see the underside. In the middle of hundreds of tattoos, I saw the word *ápizz* written on his arm.

"Thanks a lot," I said. "Now I really feel the pressure to make this place work. I don't want you to have the name of a failed restaurant on your arm forever."

I was on a high. The restaurant looked beautiful, I had my friends' and family's support; it was all falling into place. I just needed these eighteen people who were now sitting in my dining room, and would be ordering at the same time, to get really good food and service.

Since Ápizz was so small and the oven was literally part of the dining room, I didn't see the need to install one of those expensive computer systems for waiters to use when placing their orders with the kitchen. Our system was much simpler: The waiter would walk over to the oven and hand a piece of paper to Marco with his order written out. Marco would tell Lorenzo and Ian what they needed to cook and, depending on the order, get to work on his own dishes. I was standing nearby watching the process closely and looking for mistakes.

Carson came over to the oven first and handed in his order. Marco immediately started calling out dishes, some in Spanish to Lorenzo and some in a sort of hybrid of Spanish and English to Ian.

"*Dos* margherita pizza, *tres* calamari, *dos* salad, *uno* artichoke, *y tres* sausage pizza."

Right away the three cooks looked overwhelmed. Salt, pepper, and flour were flying, bread crumbs fell on the floor, and parsley was all over the counter. It was a mess.

Marcus, our other waiter, came over and handed in another ticket.

"*Tres* meatballs, *dos* lasagna, *uno* ravioli, *y uno* fish."

"What kind of fish?" Ian yelled. His face was bright red and his eyes were wild.

"*Que?*" Marco said.

"Fish, what kind of goddamn fish do you want, swordfish or whole fish?"

I ran over and looked at the ticket.

"He wants a whole fish," I said.

"Well, he should have said that," Ian grumbled. I could tell he was freaking out.

"Ian, calm down," I said. "It's our first night."

I called over Xerxes, to tell Marco in Spanish that he needed to specify the kind of fish that was being ordered.

"*Sí,*" Marco said. "I understand."

The *filone* bread, tomato sauce, and fresh ricotta cheese we had put out on the tables when people first sat down seemed to be a big hit. I heard Anthony's wife, Maureen, say, "You gotta try this; it's so good." But the real test was coming as dishes began to hit the tables. I tried to watch everyone's reaction to their first bite of food.

Most people looked really happy and a few looked sort of indifferent. But two people seemed confused. I told Pam to check with one of the confused guests while I went over to the other one.

"Is everything okay?" I asked my Aunt Patricia.

"Yeah, John, it's fine."

"Aunt Pat, what's up? Tell me."

"No, really, honey; it's fine."

"You have to tell me if something's wrong so I can fix it," I said.

"Okay. The lasagna is cold in the middle and the calamari is overcooked."

"I'm sorry," I said. "Let me bring you something else." I grabbed the dishes off the table and brought them to the back, near the dishwasher. I tasted both. Aunt Pat was right, the calamari was rubbery and the middle of the lasagna was ice cold. They were both Ian's dishes. Pam walked to the back of the restaurant holding a barely touched margherita pizza, another one of Ian's dishes.

"The dough is undercooked," she said. "But the good news is that everyone loves the whole fish; it's a huge hit."

"The whole fish better be a huge hit," I said. "It's pretty much foolproof."

More family and friends arrived and the orders kept coming in an endless stream. As the night progressed, the reactions to the food were more of the same, a mix of gushing, indifference, and yes, a few more dishes that were sent back. In the middle of it all, Xerxes told me that a writer from *Daily Candy,* an online guide to what's hot in the city, called to ask if she could stop by the next day to get some information for an item they were running on us the following Tuesday, our official opening day. I was so wrapped up in getting through the evening that it barely registered.

At the end of the night, after all of the diners and waitstaff left, I sat down with my three cooks—the two *amigos* and Ian.

"Tonight didn't work out so good," I said.

"If you don't mind me saying so," replied Ian, "I think we should change the menu. If we put more cold dishes on, it would keep the oven less crowded."

That was not the solution I was looking for. "That's not going to happen," I said.

"Okay. I guess we'll keep practicing with the oven. I think we can get it down by next week."

I saw Marco and Lorenzo exchange looks. I was already worried about the next night, when another thirty-five invited guests were coming in. I needed to figure this all out. I sent the guys home and stayed behind with Pam. We sat down at table sixteen, in the middle of the dining room, and had a glass of wine.

"I forgot to tell you," I said. *"Daily Candy* is coming by tomorrow. They're doing an item on us on Tuesday."

"Oh, my God," she said. I couldn't tell if she was excited or scared.

"What is it?"

"A *Daily Candy* item on its own will bring a lot of people here. Combine that with the *New York* magazine piece that's hitting the same day and the *Time Out* item that's running to-morrow . . . we're going to be crowded."

"And we're not ready."

"No, we're not."

I looked at our menu: eight apps, three pizzas, and eight entrées. I wrote Marco's, Lorenzo's or Ian's initials next to the dishes each was responsible for. "This is a small, simple menu," I said. "It should be manageable for these guys."

"Then what's the problem?" Pam asked.

"I think it's Ian."

"He disrupts the vibe here."

"Exactly," I said. "But more importantly, all the problem dishes tonight were his, and he has already had ten days of practice."

"Are you going to fire him before he comes in or wait till he gets here?"

"I'll call him in the morning, save him a trip downtown."

"Who's going to replace him?" Pam asked.

"I've been watching Lorenzo; he really gets the oven. I could move him over to do Ian's dishes and have Marco cook Lorenzo's hot dishes. That leaves some cold appetizers and sal-ads, which are really easy," I said. "The dressings for the salads are prepped downstairs before service."

With only three cold dishes on the menu, I kept thinking we might be able to pull it off with a two-man line. The problem tonight wasn't that each guy had too much on his plate. Lorenzo and Marco worked really well together. I would talk to them in the morning about reorganizing the dishes they were responsible for and see if tomorrow night we could man-age with just the two of them.

"I really wish I could just step in and cook," I said. "Maybe I could be the garde-manger."

"The what?" Pam asked.

"Never mind."

MY MEATBALLS
GET A MAKEOVER

IT WAS THREE DAYS before our opening, and the meatballs were still nagging at me. There was something about them that just wasn't right. I had a feeling they would be one of our most popular dishes, so they had to be really good. I asked Lorenzo and Marco to cook them over and over again, hoping they might perfect them through repetition but each time, something was off. Whenever I asked them what they thought, they gave me the same responses: Lorenzo said, "To me, it's okay," and Marco just shrugged in agreement.

I wasn't a chef but I did grow up eating great Italian meatballs, so I decided to get to the bottom of it myself. I went downstairs to the prep kitchen and watched closely as Marco

prepped the meatballs. I wrote down every step, measuring the exact amounts of salt, pepper, and bread he was using. When he was finished, I asked him to cook one in the wood-burning oven for me. I sat down in the dining room alone and cut into it. The good news was that my cooks were finally getting used to the oven; the inside of the meatball was hot and juicy. I chewed my first bite slowly, letting the meat roll around a bit in my mouth. The taste certainly wasn't terrible. Maybe a little bland, I thought. It was the consistency that was really off. These meatballs were still way too dense—more like meat loaf. I had to figure out how to make them softer and more flavorful.

I went back down to the prep kitchen, laid out all the ingredients and made several versions—some with less bread, others with less egg, or with more salt, pepper, or onions, and so on. Less than an hour later, I had five versions in front of me. I called Pam and Xerxes to come be my taste testers.

"Remember," I said, "pay attention to the flavor and the texture. Are they too loose, too heavy, too salty, not salty enough?"

We all worked from left to right, jotting down notes on each version as we ate. Fifteen minutes later, and totally full, we all agreed that version number five

The meatball experiment.
Pam and Xerxes, my lab rats,
conduct a taste test.

was the best, in both consistency and flavor. It was the one that had everything but the kitchen sink in it. This meatball had the most parsley, salt, pepper, and onions. I had even thrown in a handful of chopped basil and Parmigiano-Reggiano.

I took another bite. It was delicious—full of fresh herbs and a subtle, cheesy flavor. But I had a feeling I could still make it better.

"Wait here," I said. "I have one more for you to try."

"Dude, I can't eat another bite," Xerxes said.

"Can we just finish this tomorrow?" Pam asked.

"Tomorrow? That's a year away," I said. "I can have thirty-six more versions by tomorrow."

"Well, we can't breathe, we're so full," Pam said. "I guess we'll be having thirty-six different meatballs for breakfast tomorrow." Pam dragged Xerxes out with her and I went back to the kitchen.

OPENING NIGHT

THE DAY WE OPENED, we appeared in *New York* magazine's fall preview guide and *Daily Candy*. The next day, Florence Fabricant at the *New York Times* was going to run a second item on our opening. The week before, our write-up and photo had appeared in *Time Out New York*. There was definitely a buzz. Still, I couldn't help but worry that no one would show up to eat dinner on opening night.

The reappearance of the phone booth put me way behind schedule, and I played catch-up for the rest of the day until we opened at six o'clock. I spent one hour redecorating the counter in front of the oven with fresh fruits and vegetables, two hours lighting the liquor bottles behind the bar so they glowed just right, and three hours finishing the wood that Quang had cut to hold our menus. In the middle of it all, a huge fake plant that didn't fit at all with my décor arrived from Pam's mother.

Xerxes spent most of the day downstairs answering the phone, which rang frequently. I hoped that meant he was taking reservations and not messages from my parents wishing me luck. At three-thirty, he came upstairs to talk to me.

"We're getting pretty full for tonight," he said.

"Really?"

"Yeah, I took sixty-three reservations already."

"What?" Excitement and panic set in.

"Don't worry, I spaced them out as much as possible. We have about twenty people coming between six and seven."

That was good news, since the first hour of business was always the slowest.

"Maybe we shouldn't take any more," I said. "I would rather do less business tonight and do it right."

The energy started building at four o'clock, when our waiters, busboy, and bartender arrived. By four-thirty, Marcus and Carson were folding napkins and setting tables; José, our busboy, was lighting votives and polishing silverware; and Diego, the bartender, was setting up his speed rack at the bar and slicing lemons for drinks. Lorenzo and Marco came upstairs from the prep kitchen at about five o'clock to set up their stations. I took a break from sanding the wood for our menus and watched it all. There was no going back now, I thought.

I went over the checklist in my head. The room looked beautiful, and the fire was picking up some nice momentum in the oven. My staff seemed prepared as they reviewed their notes on each dish and bottle of wine. Marco and Lorenzo had worked out well on our second night for friends and family. They had an easy rhythm and never lost their cool. Even my meatballs were better. At the last minute, I had decided to add a creamy ricotta filling. I had Lorenzo core out their centers to make room, so we could pipe the cheese in right before they went in the oven. Yet I still worried about whether we would be good enough to wow customers. All the press would bring a lot of people in for one meal, but it was up to us to make sure they came back again. I knew tonight was our big chance.

They came in slowly at first, beginning at six-fifteen, but within an hour, the room was filled with thirty-three people, including a few walk-ins who had read about us in *New York* magazine. The crowd was totally mixed: we had Upper East Side ladies (I was shocked they had made the trek down to Eldridge Street), a few guys from Wall Street, two gay couples, and lots of stylish young women carrying a printout of the item on us from *Daily Candy*. And the most amazing thing was that I didn't know any of them. They were all strangers who came because they had read about us in the news. Seeing my place filled, for the first time, with people I didn't know will always be one of the greatest thrills for me of opening a restaurant. It made the whole thing seem real.

I studied people's expressions as they walked into the restaurant, passed the hostess stand,

and saw the dining room and oven for the first time. Would the dramatic effect I had worked so hard to achieve be lost on them? Fortunately, a lot of people acknowledged it in some way. I heard comments like, "Oh, it's lovely in here" and "What a beautiful room." I listened as Marcus and Carson spoke to customers for the first time. I wanted to know how they represented the restaurant, and what kinds of comments and questions people had. I heard a few people ask who designed the room and what was here before. Earlier in the week, I had asked Pam to write up a fact sheet on the restaurant to help the staff answer almost anything that was thrown at them.

The orders started coming in. There were only a couple of orders of swordfish, eggplant rollatini, and chicken roasted with lemon. Almost everyone seemed to want the whole fish, pizza, lasagna, or meatballs, which was fine by me. These were the dishes I felt the most confident about. We had the usual mishaps that I expected on our first night: a couple of tables had to wait longer than I would have liked for their entrées; at one table people's appetizers came out at completely different times; and one person sent back the pizza because the crust was burnt. I bought dessert for anyone who had a problem, hoping they would give us another chance. On the other hand, a lot of people seemed to be enjoying their dinners. On their way out, several diners went out of their way to say they would be back. But something was bothering me. That night wasn't terrible. The whole thing felt fine to me, but not great. And I knew I wouldn't survive on "fine." Not in New York.

A FEW WEEKS after our opening, we found out that the *New York Times* was featuring us in their weekly "Diner's Journal" column. While it's technically not a review and doesn't assign any stars, "Diner's Journal" does read like a critique of a restaurant. Unlike the safe opening announcements, the writer Eric Asimov's piece would express an opinion. Since I had no idea when he had been in and whether or not he enjoyed his meal, all I could do was hope for the best. I was a nervous wreck.

"Diner's Journal" runs on Fridays, so I was on the *Times*'s website on Thursday night at midnight, hoping to find the write-up. I was completely anxious, feeling as if my entire future would be laid out on the screen before me. I saw the photo first, a black and white shot of Lorenzo and Marco working in front of the oven. The text wasn't very long, about six short paragraphs, but the message was clear. Asimov was not impressed. The third paragraph began with, "Cooked down to its wood-burning essence, Ápizz lives by the oven and dies by the oven." I felt crushed. It was like someone had dissed my baby. Asimov thought too many dishes at Ápizz picked up the smoky flavor from the oven and essentially tasted the same. The oven, my one treasured cooking implement and my stunning design element, was becoming my biggest problem.

I sat in our bedroom for another hour, staring at the computer screen and thinking. I picked up a copy of my menu and went through each dish, wondering how it could be improved. I thought about how my guys weren't covering any of the dishes before they went in the oven. Maybe some should be sealed with foil so the smokiness from the wood wouldn't infuse the food as much. Maybe some of them needed to be prepped differently. And lots of them could benefit from different seasonings and cooking times. I needed to do with every dish what I had done with the meatballs: completely dissect the recipe and, through trial and error, come up with a better version. I had to find the time; the life of my restaurant depended on it. I looked over at Pam, sleeping a few feet away.

"Are you up?" I said loudly. "Guess who's going to be the new chef at Ápizz?"

"You?" she asked sleepily.

"Yeah, me."

Five

MY LIFE AS A CHEF

I WOKE UP the next morning sure of two things: One was that you don't just wake up one morning, say you're a chef, and actually become one on the spot. There was so much stuff I needed to understand and learn before I could pull this off. The second thing I knew was that I was hungry to learn everything and anything I could about food and cooking. I jumped out of bed and ran down to Ápizz.

Marco, who by then was working solely as our prep chef, was in the kitchen already preparing for the night. As I watched him toss handfuls of ingredients into pots and onto cutting boards, it occurred to me that we didn't really have any recipes at Ápizz. Marco had cooked some variation of most of our dishes at other restaurants and simply tweaked each one, based on what my consulting chef, Rudy, had instructed him to do. There was no way to improve upon something without a starting point. So that's where I began, writing down the existing recipes and driving Marco crazy in the process.

"Wait," I would yell to him as he was about to add salt into the sauce. "How much?"

He couldn't simply toss a fistful of chopped shallots into a simmering pan without my asking him to empty it into a measuring cup first. I was slowing him down, but I didn't care.

At the end of the first day, I had written down three complete recipes for the octopus salad, tomato sauce, and pizza dough. I decided to start with the octopus.

Google the phrase *octopus recipes,* and you'll get hundreds of opinions on how to cook perfect, tender sea creatures. I had to sort through it all and figure out what was best for the dish I envisioned serving. I was sitting at the laptop in the corner of the prep kitchen, working online and taking notes. A few recipes called for rubbing olive oil on the tentacles before braising them for two hours. Others recommended soaking it in milk before cooking or boiling it in water with a wine cork. Some websites said you had to cook it quickly, no more than two minutes, while others insisted the cooking time must be no less than two hours. By the time I had gone through the first twelve websites, I had written down about nine variations, enough for me to start experimenting. I didn't want to use up our supply of octopus for the night, so I ran over to Dean & Deluca in SoHo and bought a five-pound octopus to play around with.

Back at Ápizz, I rinsed off the long purple tentacles and laid out the body on a cutting board, the arms extending about two feet off the board. If you have never held a whole octopus before, its slimy body can be kind of scary. I found it to be pretty cool. I sliced into the tentacles, carefully separating them from the body and head. I experimented slowly and meticulously, using the prep kitchen as my lab. Nine hours later, I had cooked thirteen different versions of octopus, some differing from others by a mere minute more or less of cooking time. I needed to be precise.

I imagined the taste that I wanted. I grabbed a bunch of chopped tentacles and boiled them in water with salt, pepper, and red pepper flakes, and let it cook for an hour and a half. In the meantime, I took a small sauté pan and poured in some olive oil, balsamic vinegar, a squeeze of lemon juice, and chopped red onion. I tasted the mixture. It was good but had too much of a kick, so I added a pinch of sugar, which mellowed it nicely. I removed the octopus from the boiling water and tossed it into the sauté pan. I cooked it for no more than a minute, just enough time for the octopus to pick up the flavors of the vinaigrette. It was delicious. I wanted to turn the dish into something more substantial, so I added cherry tomatoes, celery, parsley, and some boiled potatoes, which gave the salad a hot-and-cold element that I really liked. It was nine o'clock at night, and I finally had a version that I was happy with.

Unfortunately, this was only the beginning. Now I had to take my new recipe, which was tested on a stove top, and translate it so it would work in the wood-burning oven. I started from scratch again. This time, instead of sautéing it downstairs, I brought it upstairs to the oven, which was roaring for dinner service. I thought about how I could mimic a sauté in the oven. I grabbed a small terra-cotta pot, put in some olive oil, and timed how long it would take to heat up. It took close to five minutes for the oil to bubble, giving me a seven- to seven-and-a-half-minute cooking time. Too long. It doesn't sound like a lot of time, but seven and a half minutes on a busy Saturday night when you need to get an appetizer out right away is an eternity. I grabbed one of the iron sizzle plates that Lorenzo stored near the fire and tried heating a new batch of oil on that. I got the dish in and out of the oven in two and half minutes.

The only things left to do were to teach Marco how to prep it, and Omar, our new cook, how to finish the dish when an order came in. I called Xerxes over.

"From now on, you are going to translate all the new recipes into Spanish," I said. "And tomorrow I want you to buy a laminating machine. I want every recipe laminated and clipped above Marco's cooking station downstairs."

Over the next three weeks, I would cook from nine in the morning until eleven at night, methodically breaking down every dish into its separate ingredients and reconstructing it as a better version of its former self. Afterward I would leave Ápizz and go home and study, burying my head in one of the twenty-five books on cooking I had bought recently. I had spent seven hundred and thirty dollars in one shot at Barnes & Noble. I was living and breathing food. Most nights, I was still at the kitchen table at home hitting the books when Pam kissed me goodnight. And several mornings I was right where she left me. One morning she woke up at seven, still half asleep, to find me in our kitchen surrounded by dirty pots and pans. There was olive oil, fresh basil leaves, and rosemary everywhere.

"Is there any coffee?" she mumbled.

"No, but try this ragu of wild boar."

"I don't think I can eat that right now."

"Come on, it's the breakfast of champions."

ONCE THE MENU RECIPES were refined, I spent every night during service in front of the oven with Lorenzo and Omar, not so much cooking as overseeing everything they were doing. I watched how much salt and cheese they used in a dish before putting it in the oven, checked to see if they covered the right dishes, and then made sure everything stayed in the oven for the exact amount of time I had specified in my new recipes.

The finished dining room of Ápizz

I felt like I had made the food better—up from a 3 or 4 to a 6 or 7—but I knew I still had a long way to go. I spent every minute cooking and thinking about food, but was careful never to refer to myself as a chef. I wouldn't let Pam use that title with my name attached to it when talking to the media. I needed to learn more.

Over the next few months, I gradually felt more confident. One night, I was standing on the cooking line with Omar and Lorenzo when a middle-aged couple I recognized walked in. They had been in for dinner twice the week before and three times the week before that. I wanted to send a special midcourse out to them as a thank-you for coming in so regularly, something that wasn't on the menu. I hadn't personally cooked anything for a customer yet and felt nervous about a stranger trying a dish I improvised and cooked on my own. But I felt like I was ready. That morning I had gone to Whole Foods and bought a pound of *hen of the woods* mushrooms to experiment with. As I cleaned them, I asked Lorenzo to cook a half order of our ravioli. Usually we served two large ravioli—basically two big squares of pasta each with ricotta and Parmigiano in the middle, sort of like a sandwich.

"Mix just a little chopped thyme into the cheese," I said. *"Poco."*

While he placed a scoop of the cheese in between the pasta, I put some butter in a sauté pan, threw in some chopped shallots and garlic along with a sprig of thyme, tossed in my mushrooms and salt and pepper, and slid the pan in the oven. My movements felt natural now after cooking for so many weeks downstairs. When I removed the pan, the savory smell of warm butter and simmering garlic immediately filled the restaurant. I tasted a mushroom. It was really good, an earthy, nutty flavor with a subtle hint of thyme. But it needed something. I grabbed a lemon off the counter and cut it in half. I squeezed the juice over the mushrooms and mixed them up a bit. I tasted another one. This time it was perfect; the lemon juice made all the flavors jump and come to life. I loved it. Lorenzo placed one large raviolo on a plate, and I poured the mushrooms on top. I laid a fresh sprig of thyme on the side of the plate as a garnish and sent it over to the couple.

I watched for any reaction after they took their first bites. The woman was facing the oven, so I could see her well. She chewed slowly, closing her eyes as she kept her empty fork near her mouth. Then she opened her eyes and from across the room I saw her mouth the words, "Oh, my God, this is so good."

"Yesss," I whispered to myself. I was on a high from that reaction.

I couldn't have known it at the time, but months later my meatballs would be rated among the top five in the city by *New York* magazine, and Hal Rubenstein, their restaurant critic, would name Ápizz the best place to impress a foodie. Diners would rave about our polenta and pork chops online. But seeing that woman mouth those words after trying my food will always remain one of the biggest thrills of my cooking career.

As the couple left the restaurant, they stopped by the cooking line to thank me.

"Are you the chef?" the woman asked.

"Uh, no," I said.

"Well, those mushrooms were to die for," she said.

Over the next few weeks, I practiced making new dishes that weren't on the menu. My cooking became much more spontaneous as I felt more comfortable in the kitchen and didn't need to rely on recipes anymore. I made daily trips to Whole Foods to buy ingredients I had never cooked with before—things like foie gras, fresh anchovies, and sweetbreads—and experimented with different cooking techniques. I made polenta cakes topped with chanterelles, osso buco, potato gnocchi with braised short ribs, and beef carpaccio. I sent out small plates of each new creation to our regular diners, who seemed to love the food.

One night, more than six months after I had first decided to teach myself to cook, I was standing on the line with Lorenzo and Omar. The three of us were wearing chef's whites and working on different dishes. The dining room was busy, and there was a sea of terra-cotta pots in the oven. On his way out, a guy in his mid-thirties stopped by the oven to talk to us. He was rubbing his stomach to show how full he was.

"Wow, that was a great meal," he said.

We all said, "Thank you."

"Who's the chef?" he asked.

Omar and Lorenzo both looked at me.

"I am," I said with a smile.

PART II

RECIPES

~

Six

APPETIZERS
& ANTIPASTI

PEPPER-CRUSTED BEEF CARPACCIO

4 to 6 servings

This is a great light appetizer. We serve it at Ápizz during the summer months with an arugula salad and shaved Parmesan. It also works well in a sandwich with hard, crusty bread and roasted peppers.

For the carpaccio:

1½ tablespoons whole black peppercorns

1½ teaspoons salt

12 ounces boneless prime top round

1½ tablespoons olive oil

For the salad:

4 to 6 cups arugula

2 tablespoons red wine vinegar

6 tablespoons extra-virgin olive oil

Salt and black pepper to taste

(Continued)

1. To make the carpaccio, use a rolling pin to lightly crush the peppercorns between two sheets of wax paper until they are flattened and broken into coarse pieces. Mix the pepper and salt together in a small mixing bowl and sprinkle over a flat work surface.

2. Roll the meat in the salt and pepper until all the surfaces are well covered.

3. Coat the bottom of a small sauté pan with the olive oil. Heat over high heat until it begins to smoke. Put the meat in the pan and sear all sides until browned, about 20 to 30 seconds per side. Remove the meat from the pan and allow it to cool for 10 minutes. Wrap it tightly in plastic wrap and store in the freezer for 2 hours. Before serving, unwrap the meat, and let it sit for 10 to 15 minutes.

4. Meanwhile, make the salad. In a medium mixing bowl, toss the arugula, vinegar, extra-virgin olive oil, salt, and pepper together.

5. Using a very sharp knife, cut the meat into paper-thin slices. To serve, line the edges of four to six 8-inch salad plates with the carpaccio. Mound some of the arugula salad in the center of each plate.

FRENCH GREEN BEANS SAUTÉED WITH TOMATOES AND BASIL

6 servings

*This appetizer tastes so fresh, you can almost substitute it for a salad.
Using French green beans also gives it a sophisticated twist.*

3 tablespoons extra-virgin olive oil

1 cup finely chopped onion

2 garlic cloves, minced

1½ pounds French green beans *(haricots verts)*, ends trimmed to make a uniform size

1½ teaspoons salt

Pinch of black pepper

1 cup sliced cherry tomatoes

1 cup packed fresh basil leaves

1. Heat the olive oil in a large nonstick skillet over medium heat until it just begins to smoke. Add the onion and garlic and sauté until the onions soften slightly, about 5 minutes.

2. Add the green beans, salt, pepper, and ½ cup of water. Cook until the beans are tender yet crisp, about 10 minutes. Add the tomatoes and basil and cook for an additional 3 minutes, until the tomatoes begin to soften. Serve hot or at room temperature.

STEAMED CLAMS WITH CHORIZO

4 servings

This is one of those really flavorful, brothy dishes that you can't wait to dunk a big piece of crusty bread into. There is something about the tomatoes and fresh herbs that make this recipe feel summery, but the truth is that it's great all year round. My favorite thing about this dish is the chorizo, which gives it just the right amount of spice.

1½ to 2½ tablespoons olive oil

2 baking potatoes, peeled and cut into ½-inch cubes

1 red bell pepper, diced

½ onion, roughly chopped

Pinch of salt plus 1 tablespoon

Pinch of black pepper

1 chorizo sausage (about 4 ounces)

24 fresh littleneck clams

1 cup fresh lemon juice (about 4 lemons)

¾ cup dry white wine

2 cups chicken stock

2 tablespoons sugar

1 cup halved yellow grape tomatoes

1 cup halved red grape tomatoes

3 garlic cloves, chopped

½ cup chopped fresh cilantro

½ cup roughly chopped fresh basil

½ cup chopped fresh parsley

1. Coat the bottom of a large stockpot with the olive oil. Heat the oil over medium heat until it begins to smoke. Add the potatoes, red pepper, onions, and a pinch of salt and pepper and cook until the potatoes begin to brown, 10 to 15 minutes.

2. Cut the chorizo into twenty ¼-inch slices. Add the sausage, the remaining tablespoon of salt, and the remaining ingredients to the pot. Once the liquid comes to a boil, cover the pot to let the clams steam open and the alcohol burn off, 8 to 10 minutes.

3. Divide the clams and chorizo among 4 bowls (discard the clams that don't open). Using a large spoon or ladle, cover the clams with the broth and vegetables. Serve immediately.

SHRIMP AND CHORIZO WITH CRISPY GARLIC CHIPS

4 servings

There's a lot going on in this dish, and it's all good. The chorizo and garlic chips really bring the shrimp to life. But the best thing about this is the savory oil you're left with at the end. Grab a piece of bread and start dunking.

For the garlic chips:

½ cup olive oil

4 garlic cloves, thinly sliced

¼ cup all-purpose flour

Salt to taste

For the shrimp:

1 chorizo sausage (about 4 ounces)

2 tablespoons butter

16 jumbo shrimp, peeled and deveined, with tails intact

Olive oil

½ cup Herbed Bread Crumbs (page 195) or store-bought Italian seasoned bread crumbs

1½ teaspoons salt

Pinch of black pepper

2 teaspoons chopped fresh thyme

2 teaspoons chopped fresh parsley

1. To make the garlic chips, in a small skillet, heat the olive oil to 350°F over medium-high heat. In the meantime, toss the garlic slices in flour until they are well coated. Put the garlic in the oil and cook until golden brown, about 3 minutes. Remove from the pan and put them on a paper towel to drain. Sprinkle with salt and set aside.

2. To make the shrimp, cut the chorizo into twenty ¼-inch slices and set aside. Melt the butter in a medium saucepan over medium heat. Add the shrimp to the pan and toss well to coat them evenly in butter. Cook until they just begin to turn light pink, about 1 minute. Add enough olive oil to the pan to cover the shrimp about three-quarters of the way. Add the bread crumbs in an even layer. Add the salt, pepper, chorizo, thyme, and parsley. Bring the mixture to a gentle boil, lower the heat, and simmer 4 to 6 minutes, turning the shrimp over after 2 minutes.

3. To serve, use a slotted spoon to put 5 slices of chorizo and 4 shrimp in each of 4 small bowls. Spoon the oil from the pan over the shrimp to form a ½-inch-deep puddle at the bottom of each bowl. Toss the crispy garlic chips over the shrimp and serve immediately.

BERRY CHUTNEY

12 servings

*This berry chutney is a perfect accompaniment for Cured Beef Tenderloin (page 100).
I like to serve it as an hors d'oeuvre with butterhead lettuce. I use a whole lettuce leaf
as the vehicle for each serving and place a round piece of beef tenderloin,
about ⅛ inch thick, in the middle of the lettuce. I finish it off by drizzling
1½ teaspoons of chutney down the center and garnishing
the dish with loose berries.*

1½ tablespoons butter

½ cup tawny port wine

¼ cup blackberries, sliced in half

½ cup raspberries, sliced in half

2½ teaspoons sugar

2½ teaspoons salt

Pinch of black pepper

½ teaspoon ground coriander

½ cup mayonnaise, preferably Hellmann's

2½ tablespoons prepared minced horseradish

2 tablespoons Dijon mustard

2 tablespoons chopped fresh mint

1 tablespoon fresh lemon juice

1½ teaspoons Worcestershire sauce

1. In a small saucepan over medium heat, melt the butter until the foam begins to subside, about 3 minutes.

2. Add the port to the pan and cook for 5 minutes to reduce the liquid. Add the berries, sugar, salt, pepper, and coriander. Lightly mash the berries with a spoon as you stir the mixture. Lower the heat and let the mixture simmer for 5 minutes. Remove from the heat and allow to cool to room temperature.

3. In a medium bowl, mix together the mayonnaise, horseradish, mustard, mint, lemon juice, and Worcestershire. Add the berry mixture to the bowl and mix well. The berry chutney can be refrigerated for up to 3 days before using.

MARINATED TOMATOES

4 to 6 servings

There is nothing more summery than red and yellow tomatoes and fresh herbs. This dish smells as good as it looks. It's also versatile—we serve it on its own as a salad, poured over grilled steak, or alongside steamed lobster.

2 cups red grape tomatoes (one 10-ounce package)
2 cups yellow grape tomatoes (one 10-ounce package)
1 shallot, finely chopped
½ cup extra-virgin olive oil
¼ cup balsamic vinegar
¼ cup chopped fresh basil
¼ cup chopped fresh parsley
2 tablespoons chopped fresh mint
1½ teaspoons salt
¼ teaspoon black pepper

1. Cut the tomatoes in half and put them in a medium mixing bowl. Add the remaining ingredients and mix well.

2. Cover the bowl with plastic wrap and let the mixture marinate in the refrigerator for at least 30 minutes or up to 24 hours before serving. Serve cold or at room temperature.

CORN RELISH

4 servings

This is one of my most versatile recipes—it goes well with so many things. Over the years, I have served it as an appetizer, as part of an antipasto, as a side dish to grilled pork chops, and alongside rib-eye steak. It's great warm or cold.

4 ears fresh sweet corn
4 tablespoons butter
4 teaspoons olive oil
½ cup chopped shallots
¾ cup diced red bell pepper
¾ cup roughly chopped cremini mushroom caps
¼ cup chopped fresh cilantro
¼ cup chopped fresh basil
¼ cup chopped fresh parsley
4 teaspoons white vinegar
Salt and black pepper to taste

1. Remove the husks and silk from the corn and discard. Boil the corn in a large stockpot of rapidly boiling water for 10 minutes. Remove the corn from the pot and allow it to cool for a few minutes before handling. Cut the kernels off of each ear with a small knife and set aside. (You should have about 2 cups.)

2. Heat the butter and olive oil in a medium saucepan over medium heat. Add the shallots and cook until tender, about 3 minutes. Add the pepper and cook for 2 minutes. Add the mushrooms and cook for an additional 2 minutes. If the mixture becomes too dry, add 1½ teaspoons of butter.

3. Stir in the corn, cilantro, basil, and parsley and cook for 1 minute. Remove the pan from the heat and pour the mixture into a medium mixing bowl. Add the vinegar and mix well. Season with salt and pepper.

LENTILS WITH OVEN-ROASTED PLUM TOMATOES AND BALSAMIC GLAZE

6 servings

When I discovered black beluga lentils, I knew I had to create a dish for them. They are smaller and rounder than typical green lentils, and their black color creates a stark contrast on the plate. For this dish, the balsamic glaze adds a nice sweetness that balances the acidity of the tomatoes. At Ápizz we serve this as an appetizer, but the lentils would work well as a side dish for fish or seafood.

For the balsamic glaze:

1½ cups aged balsamic vinegar from Modena

1 tablespoon sugar

For the lentils:

1½ to 2 tablespoons olive oil

5 garlic cloves

½ cup roughly chopped onion

½ cup chopped carrots

½ cup chopped celery

8 sprigs fresh thyme

1½ teaspoons sugar

1 tablespoon salt

1½ teaspoons black pepper

2 tablespoons sherry vinegar

1½ cups black beluga lentils, rinsed

Oven-Roasted Plum Tomatoes (recipe follows)

1. To make the glaze, combine the balsamic vinegar and sugar in a small saucepan over very low heat. Simmer until the mixture is reduced to ½ cup, 40 to 50 minutes. Remove from the heat and refrigerate, uncovered, for 1 to 2 hours.

2. To make the lentils, heat the olive oil in a medium saucepan over medium heat until it just begins to smoke. (Use enough oil to coat the bottom of the pan.) Meanwhile, smash the garlic with the flat side of a large knife. Add the garlic and all the remaining ingredients, except the lentils, to the pan and cook until the vegetables sweat, 10 to 15 minutes. Pour in 6 cups of water, cover, bring to a boil, reduce the heat, and simmer for 1 hour.

3. Strain the mixture, pouring the liquid into a measuring cup and return the vegetables to the saucepan. You should have about 4½ cups of liquid.

4. Rinse the lentils in cold water and pour them into the saucepan with the vegetables. Add 2 cups of the strained liquid to the pan and bring to a boil. Reduce the heat and simmer until the liquid is almost completely absorbed, 8 to 10 minutes. Add another 2 cups of liquid and repeat the process. Taste the lentils; they should be cooked until tender yet firm. If they are not done, add the remaining ½ cup of liquid and cook until it's fully absorbed.

5. Divide the lentils among 6 small dinner plates, forming a mound in the center of each one. Surround the lentils with the plum tomatoes, and drizzle each serving with 1½ teaspoons of the balsamic glaze.

OVEN-ROASTED PLUM TOMATOES

4 to 6 servings

This is one of the simplest—and most foolproof—dishes you can make. We serve it with the black lentils on page 96 or with Parmigiano-Reggiano and homemade bread sticks.

6 plum tomatoes, cut into quarters
1½ tablespoons salt
1½ teaspoons black pepper
1½ teaspoons sugar
1½ teaspoons dried oregano
1 tablespoon chopped fresh parsley
10 sprigs fresh thyme
6 basil leaves, torn into small pieces

1. Preheat the oven to 250°F. Remove the seeds and most of the flesh from the tomatoes, so you're left with pieces about ¼ inch thick.

2. Place the tomatoes, skin-side down, on a baking sheet. Sprinkle evenly with the salt, pepper, sugar, oregano, and parsley. Toss the thyme sprigs and basil leaves over the tomatoes. Bake, un-covered, until well roasted and dry, 1 to 1¼ hours. Serve warm or at room temperature.

CHERRY TOMATO AND POTATO SALAD WITH CRISPY PROSCIUTTO AND MUSTARD VINAIGRETTE

6 servings

Here is a great Italian alternative to traditional potato salad. The crispy prosciutto and chopped celery add a crunchy texture, which I love alongside soft potatoes. This salad is beautiful when served warm, as soon as you're done cooking. But it's also great the next day, after it has sat in the refrigerator overnight, and the potatoes have had a chance to absorb all the flavors.

2 pounds potatoes, peeled and cut into ¼-inch dice

2 tablespoons butter

4 ounces sliced prosciutto, chopped

½ cup chopped red onion

1½ cups sliced cherry tomatoes

1 cup chopped celery

¼ cup chopped fresh chives

4 to 5 tablespoons Red Wine and Dijon Mustard Vinaigrette (page 194)

1. Put the potatoes in a large saucepan with 2½ cups of salted water, and bring to a boil. Reduce the heat to medium and cook until the potatoes are just tender, 8 to 10 minutes. Drain and place in a large bowl to cool.

2. Melt the butter in a medium nonstick skillet over medium heat. Add the prosciutto and sauté until crisp, 6 to 8 minutes. At the last minute, add the onion, tomatoes, and celery and toss to coat well. Remove the mixture from the heat.

3. Pour the prosciutto mixture over the potatoes. Add the vinaigrette to taste and mix well. Serve warm or chilled.

CURED BEEF TENDERLOIN

12 servings

I serve this dish at Ápizz with Berry Chutney (page 92) because the sweetness of the berries offsets the strong flavors of the horseradish, vinegar, and red pepper. I also love this beef tenderloin on a sandwich with horseradish mayo. The beef needs to cure for at least 12 hours, and will keep for one week in the fridge.

1 cup salt

½ cup sugar

2 tablespoons black pepper

1 teaspoon red pepper flakes

1 teaspoon garlic powder

1 teaspoon onion powder

½ cup red wine

½ cup fresh lemon juice

2 cups olive oil

2 tablespoons prepared horseradish

½ cup balsamic vinegar

½ red bell pepper, diced

1 cup halved cherry tomatoes

2 cups chopped fresh basil, loosely packed

½ cup chopped fresh mint, loosely packed

1 cup chopped fresh thyme, loosely packed

1 cup chopped fresh rosemary, loosely packed

One 1¼ to 1½ pounds beef tenderloin

Toasted Italian bread for serving

1. In a large saucepan over medium heat, combine all the ingredients except the beef tenderloin and bread. Heat the mixture until the salt and sugar dissolve and the herbs wilt slightly, about 5 minutes (the liquid should not boil). Remove the pan from the heat.

2. Put the beef tenderloin in a casserole dish or pan about 2½ inches deep, 6 inches wide, and 12 inches long. Cover the beef with the entire herb mixture. If the beef is not fully covered, add enough olive oil so it's fully submerged in liquid. Wrap the pan tightly with plastic wrap and refrigerate for at least 12 hours and up to 2 days.

3. Cut the beef into paper-thin slices. To serve, line the outer edges of salad plates with the beef. Place a mound of berry chutney in the center. Serve with small slices of toasted bread.

SALMON TARTARE WITH POTATO CRISPS AND RED ONION CRÈME FRAÎCHE

8 servings

This version of salmon tartare is unusually flavorful, with the citrus and red onion really popping in every bite. The fried potatoes should be extremely crispy in order to hold the tartare. Feel free to substitute tuna or yellowtail for the salmon—just be sure to buy superior-quality fish.

For the salmon marinade:

1½ cups olive oil

½ cup fresh lemon juice

¼ cup fresh lime juice

6 tablespoons chopped fresh chives

6 tablespoons chopped red onion

2 tablespoons salt

Black pepper to taste

For the red onion crème fraîche:

1½ tablespoons chopped red onion

½ teaspoon salt

8 ounces crème fraîche

For the potato crisps:

2 baking potatoes, peeled and cubed

1 teaspoon chopped fresh chives,

1 teaspoon chopped fresh parsley

Salt and black pepper to taste

1 cup all-purpose flour plus additional for rolling out dough

1 cup vegetable oil

2 pounds salmon fillet, skinned and cut into ⅛-inch dice

1. Prepare the salmon marinade first. In a large mixing bowl, whisk together all the ingredients. (The salmon will be added right before serving.) Cover the bowl with plastic wrap and store in the refrigerator.

2. To make the red onion crème fraîche, in a small mixing bowl, fold the red onion and salt into the crème fraîche. Cover the bowl with plastic wrap and store in the refrigerator until serving.

3. To make the potato crisps, put the potatoes in a small pot of water. Bring the water to a boil and cook until the potatoes are fork-tender, 10 to 15 minutes. Remove from the water and run them through a ricer or cheese grater until their consistency is soft and pulplike. In a large mixing bowl, combine the potatoes, chives, parsley, salt, and pepper. Gradually add enough of the flour to form a dough that can be shaped into a ball with your hands. On a floured work surface, roll out the dough until it is paper thin (for best results, roll it out between two sheets of wax paper), adding more flour frequently to prevent the dough from sticking to the rolling pin. Cut the dough into 3-inch-wide strips.

4. Heat the vegetable oil in a medium skillet over medium heat until it just begins to smoke. Add the potato strips and fry until very crispy, 2 to 3 minutes on each side. Place the potato strips on paper towels for 1 minute to drain.

5. In the meantime, add the salmon to the marinade and mix well.

6. To serve, place a potato crisp on each plate, top with a large spoonful of salmon tartare, and cover with a second potato crisp. Place a dollop of red onion crème fraîche on top of each crisp.

MARINATED ROASTED PEPPERS

4 servings

These are an absolute must on any antipasto plate. We use them so often at Ápizz, we make a big batch almost every day.

For the roasted peppers:
- 1 yellow bell pepper
- 1 red bell pepper
- 1 orange bell pepper

For the marinade:
- ¼ cup oil
- ¼ cup white vinegar
- 1½ teaspoons salt
- ½ teaspoon black pepper
- 2 tablespoons chopped fresh basil

1. Preheat the oven to 375°F. To roast the peppers, put them on a baking sheet and bake for 20 to 25 minutes, or until they just begin to blacken.

2. Put the peppers in a medium mixing bowl. Cover the bowl with plastic wrap and let the peppers sit for 15 to 20 minutes to loosen the skins.

3. Carefully peel the skins off the peppers and remove the core and seeds. Using a knife or your hands, break open the peppers and lay them flat on a cutting surface. Cut the peppers into ¼-inch-thick slivers.

4. Combine all the marinade ingredients in a medium mixing bowl. Toss the peppers in the marinade and let them sit for 1 to 2 hours before serving.

BUFFALO MOZZARELLA, TOMATO, AND ANCHOVY CROSTINI

8 to 10 servings

While I love the taste of anchovies, I tend to use a light hand with them when cooking. They can easily overpower a dish. This recipe calls for just a little bit of anchovy paste, which gives the crostini a nice jolt of flavor.

2 tablespoons butter

2 teaspoons anchovy paste

1 tablespoon milk

1 pound fresh buffalo mozzarella cheese, thinly sliced (reserve 2 tablespoons of the water it is packed in)

1 loaf crusty Italian bread, cut into ½ inch-thick slices

2 tablespoons extra-virgin olive oil

Salt and black pepper to taste

2 large beefsteak tomatoes, thinly sliced

2 tablespoons chopped fresh basil

1. Preheat the broiler. In a small saucepan over low heat, combine the butter, anchovy paste, milk, and the 2 tablespoons of reserved mozzarella water. Cook until the butter has melted, the paste has dissolved, and the ingredients are well combined, about 3 minutes (do not boil). Set aside.

2. Place the bread slices on a baking sheet. Brush one side of each piece with olive oil and sprinkle with salt and pepper. Top each piece with a slice of mozzarella. Broil until the cheese just starts to melt, 2 to 3 minutes. Transfer the crostini to a platter. Place 1 slice of tomato on each crostini, drizzle with anchovy sauce, and sprinkle with fresh basil.

MARGHERITA PIZZA

2 to 3 servings

We serve our pizzas at Ápizz as appetizers, which are great for two or three people to share. We prebake our dough before the beginning of service, which allows us to get the crust really crispy and cuts down on the cooking time considerably (a good thing when we get slammed).

One 16 x 6-inch Prebaked Pizza Crust at room temperature (page 198)
3 ounces buffalo mozzarella, cut into ½-inch cubes
4 to 5 tablespoons Pizza Sauce (page 197)
3 fresh basil leaves, roughly chopped

1. Preheat the oven to 500°F. Distribute the cheese evenly over the pizza crust, leaving a ¼-inch border. Spread the sauce evenly over the cheese. Bake for 3 to 4 minutes, or until the cheese begins to bubble lightly.

2. Cut the pizza in half lengthwise and crosswise. Cut the quarters in half again to make 8 slices. Sprinkle with fresh basil and serve.

PIZZA BIANCA

2 to 3 servings

In New York we refer to this as white pizza *because there is no red sauce, and the ricotta cheese is milky white. I order a "slice of white" every time I walk into a pizza place in the city, something that happens at least three times a week. At Ápizz we use buffalo mozzarella from Naples, which is driven to the restaurant in a Styrofoam crate, straight from the airport.*

One 16 x 6-inch Prebaked Pizza Crust (page 198) at room temperature
¼ cup fresh ricotta cheese
2 ounces buffalo mozzarella, cut into ½-inch cubes
2 tablespoons grated Parmigiano-Reggiano cheese
1 tablespoon olive oil
1 tablespoon chopped fresh parsley

1. Preheat the oven to 500°F. Spread the ricotta evenly over the pizza crust, leaving a ¼-inch border. Distribute the mozzarella cheese evenly over the ricotta. Sprinkle the Parmigiano-Reggiano evenly over the mozzarella.

2. Bake for 3 to 4 minutes, or until the cheese begins to bubble lightly. Cut the pizza down the middle lengthwise and crosswise. Cut each quarter in half to make 8 slices. Drizzle olive oil over the tops and finish with a sprinkling of parsley.

MOM'S EGGPLANT
IN TOMATO SAUCE

6 servings

This recipe comes straight from my mom's kitchen. Her fried eggplant is great because she takes the time to draw all the bitterness out with salt. This step also ensures that her eggplant is never watery (the kiss of death to any eggplant dish, in my opinion). Mom's eggplant is a fixture on her Sunday table; I always take a batch home with me for sandwiches during the week.

2½ pounds eggplant, peeled and cut into ¼-inch slices

1 to 1½ tablespoons salt

3 eggs

3 cups plain, store-bought bread crumbs

2 tablespoons olive oil

½ cup vegetable oil

6 to 8 cups Basic Tomato Sauce (page 197)

½ cup grated Pecorino Romano cheese

1. Preheat the oven to 350°F. Lay the eggplant slices on paper towels in one layer. Sprinkle the salt on top of the eggplant to draw out the bitterness and excess liquid. Let the eggplant sit for 20 to 30 minutes. Pat the slices dry with another paper towel to absorb the moisture that forms on top.

2. Whisk the eggs in a small mixing bowl. Pour the bread crumbs onto a flat plate. Dip each slice of eggplant in the egg mixture and then in the bread crumbs until the eggplant is well coated.

3. In a large skillet over medium-high heat, pour enough vegetable oil to cover the bottom of the pan and come about ⅛ inch up the sides. Heat the oil until it is very hot (if you can measure the temperature, it should be about 375°F). Place a few eggplant slices in the pan, without overlapping. Fry the eggplant until it is golden brown, about 1 minute on each side. Once the first batch is done, remove the slices from the pan with tongs and transfer them to a plate covered with paper towels to drain. Replenish the oil as needed and allow it to get very hot before repeating the process with more eggplant.

4. Pour a layer of tomato sauce into an 8 x 11-inch baking dish, so that it covers the bottom completely. Add a layer of eggplant slices to cover the sauce. Spread more tomato sauce over the eggplant slices and sprinkle with 1 to 1½ tablespoons of cheese. Repeat the layers until all the eggplant slices have been used. Top the last layer with sauce and cheese and bake for 20 minutes, or until the cheese is melted and the sauce is bubbly.

Seven

SOUPS

ARTICHOKE BISQUE

4 servings

*My wife loves artichokes, and this is one of her favorite soups. She insists that
I make it every Thanksgiving. Since the recipe calls for jarred
artichoke hearts, this soup can be made year-round.*

2 tablespoons butter

2 tablespoons diced shallots

1 teaspoon diced garlic

½ cup diced potatoes (½-inch dice)

2 teaspoons salt

½ teaspoon black pepper

1½ teaspoons chopped fresh cilantro

3 cups artichoke hearts (use jarred artichoke hearts, packed in water)

6 cups Vegetable Stock (page 196)

1½ teaspoons sugar

¼ cup heavy cream

2 teaspoons crème fraîche

1 tablespoon chopped fresh parsley

(Continued)

1. In a 2½-quart soup pot over low heat, melt the butter with the shallots and garlic and cook until the shallots and garlic begin to soften, about 3 minutes.

2. Add the potatoes, salt, pepper, and cilantro, and cook until the potatoes soften and brown slightly, about 8 minutes.

3. Add the artichokes, 5 cups of vegetable stock, and the sugar and mix well. Cover the pot and bring the soup to a gentle boil. Lower the heat and simmer for 15 minutes.

4. Set the soup aside to cool for a few minutes. Remove 4 of the artichoke hearts and reserve for garnishing. Working in batches, pour the soup into a blender and blend until smooth, about 15 seconds for each batch. Add the remaining vegetable stock if the mixture is too thick. Pour the soup back into the pot, add the heavy cream, and bring it to a gentle boil. Reduce the heat, simmer for 2 minutes, and remove from the heat. Stir in the crème fraîche.

5. Divide the soup among 4 soup bowls. To garnish, sprinkle with the parsley and place 1 artichoke heart in each bowl.

BUTTERNUT SQUASH SOUP WITH HONEY CREAM

4 servings

I came upon this soup by accident. One day when I was playing around with the recipe for Ápizz's open ravioli with butternut squash, I overcooked some of the squash. I didn't want to throw it away, so instead I tossed it in the blender. The puree was rich and flavorful, and it was easy to see how it would make a great soup. We serve this at Ápizz as a special during the fall months. In November diners seem to love any dish made with butternut squash.

3 tablespoons butter

½ cup chopped onion

1 teaspoon chopped garlic

4 cups peeled cubed butternut squash (½-inch cubes)

1 tablespoon salt

½ teaspoon black pepper

2 teaspoons brown sugar

½ teaspoon ground cinnamon

1 tablespoon chopped fresh sage

5 cups Vegetable Stock (page 196)

¼ cup heavy cream

1 teaspoon honey

(Continued)

1. In a 2½-quart soup pot over low heat, melt the butter with the onions and garlic and cook until they begin to soften, about 3 minutes. Add the squash, salt, pepper, brown sugar, cinnamon, and sage and cook, covered, until the squash begins to soften, 10 to 12 minutes.

2. Remove 16 squash cubes for garnishing and set aside. Add 4 cups of the vegetable stock to the mixture. Raise the heat to high and cook, uncovered, until the liquid boils. Lower the heat slightly and simmer for 10 minutes.

3. Set the soup aside to cool for a few minutes. Working in batches, pour the soup into a blender and blend until smooth, about 15 seconds for each batch. Add more vegetable stock if the soup is too thick. Add more salt and pepper to taste.

4. In a small mixing bowl, combine the heavy cream and honey.

5. Pour the soup into 4 bowls. Place 4 butternut squash cubes in the center of each bow. Drizzle a swirl of the honey cream across the top of each soup before serving.

FRENCH GREEN BEAN AND PARMESAN SOUP

4 servings

This soup is as pretty as it is delicious, which makes it great for a dinner party. I served it at my wedding in shot glasses as an hors d'oeuvre and it was a big hit. Parmigiano-Reggiano—a fine aged cheese—gives the soup a robust flavor.

2½ tablespoons butter

2 teaspoons chopped garlic

12 ounces French green beans *(haricots verts),* ends trimmed

1 teaspoon salt

¼ teaspoon black pepper

4 cups Vegetable Stock (page 196)

¼ cup heavy cream

¼ cup grated Parmigiano-Reggiano cheese, plus extra for garnish

1 tablespoon chopped fresh parsley

(Continued)

1. In a 2½-quart soup pot over low heat, melt the butter with the garlic and cook until the garlic softens, about 3 minutes. Add the green beans, salt, and pepper to the pot. Cover the pot, raise the heat to medium, and cook for 8 minutes, stirring occasionally. Remove 16 beans and set aside for garnishing.

2. Add the vegetable stock to the pot, raise the heat to high, and bring the liquid to a boil. Lower the heat slightly and simmer for 12 minutes.

3. Set the soup aside to cool for a few minutes. Working in batches, pour the soup into a blender and blend until smooth, about 15 seconds for each batch.

4. Return the soup to the pot, add the cream and cheese, and stir well. Over medium heat, return the soup to a boil. Lower the heat and simmer for 2 minutes.

5. Divide the soup among 4 bowls. Float 4 green beans in the center of each bowl, and sprinkle with cheese and parsley before serving.

LENTIL, CRISPY PANCETTA, AND WILTED ARUGULA SOUP

4 to 6 servings

*This savory favorite is perfect in the winter. It's hearty and can be a meal in itself.
The pancetta imparts a beautiful smoky flavor, while the arugula
adds a subtle bitterness.*

6 cups Vegetable Stock (page 196)

1¼ cups green lentils, rinsed

2 teaspoons salt

½ teaspoons black pepper

2 tablespoons olive oil

½ cup chopped pancetta (¼-inch pieces)

2 tablespoons diced shallots

1 cup lightly packed arugula leaves, roughly chopped

2 tablespoons crème fraîche

(Continued)

1. In a 2½-quart soup pot over high heat, combine the vegetable stock, lentils, salt, and pepper and bring to a boil. Reduce the heat to medium and simmer, uncovered, until the lentils are tender, about 20 minutes.

2. Transfer 2 cups of the mixture, including both lentils and broth, to a blender. Blend until smooth, about 15 seconds. Pour the blended mixture back into the soup pot. Keep the soup on low heat while you prepare the pancetta and arugula.

3. Heat the olive oil in a medium sauté pan over medium heat until it begins to shimmer, 2 to 4 minutes. Add the pancetta and cook until it begins to brown and crisp slightly, 3 to 5 minutes. Add the shallots and cook for 2 minutes. Add the arugula and cook until all the leaves wilt, about 2 minutes. Remove ¼ cup of the arugula from the pan for garnishing.

4. Add the pancetta, the remaining arugula, and the crème fraîche to the soup and stir well. Ladle the soup into 4 bowls, top with the reserved arugula, and serve.

PORCINI MUSHROOM AND WHITE TRUFFLE OIL SOUP

4 servings

We save this elegant soup for special occasions. The white truffle oil adds a decadent finish and distinct flavor to the dish. I recommend starting out with a small amount of truffle oil and adding more according to your taste.

2 tablespoons butter

½ cup diced shallots

1 teaspoon chopped garlic

½ cup peeled and cubed potatoes (½-inch pieces)

3 cups chopped fresh porcini mushrooms (½-inch pieces)

½ cup chopped fresh cremini mushrooms (½-inch pieces)

2 teaspoons salt

½ teaspoons black pepper

1½ teaspoons chopped fresh parsley, plus extra for garnish

1½ teaspoons fresh thyme leaves

5 cups Vegetable Stock (page 196)

¼ cup heavy cream

½ to 1 teaspoon white truffle oil

(Continued)

1. In a 2½-quart soup pot over low heat, melt the butter with the shallots and garlic and cook until they soften, about 3 minutes. Raise the heat to medium, add the potatoes, and cook until they soften and brown slightly, about 8 minutes. Add all the mushrooms, salt, pepper, parsley, and thyme. Cover the pot and cook for 6 minutes, stirring occasionally.

2. Add 4 cups of the vegetable stock to the pot. Raise the heat to high and bring to a boil. Reduce the heat to low and let the soup simmer, uncovered, for 12 minutes.

3. Set the soup aside to cool for a few minutes. Working in batches, pour the soup into a blender and blend until smooth, about 30 seconds for each batch.

4. Return the soup to the pot and keep warm until you're ready to serve. The soup can be refrigerated at this point for up to 2 days.

5. To finish the soup, add the heavy cream to the pot and simmer over medium heat for 2 minutes. If the soup is too thick, add more vegetable stock to thin it out. Stir in the truffle oil and additional salt and pepper to taste before serving.

VEAL, BEEF, AND PORK MEATBALLS
WITH RICOTTA FILLING

SHRIMP AND CHORIZO WITH CRISPY GARLIC CHIPS

OVEN-BAKED SKATE WITH
ROSEMARY-ROASTED POTATOES

FRENCH GREEN BEAN AND
PARMESAN SOUP
and
BUTTERNUT SQUASH SOUP
WITH HONEY CREAM

OVEN-ROASTED WHOLE STRIPED BASS

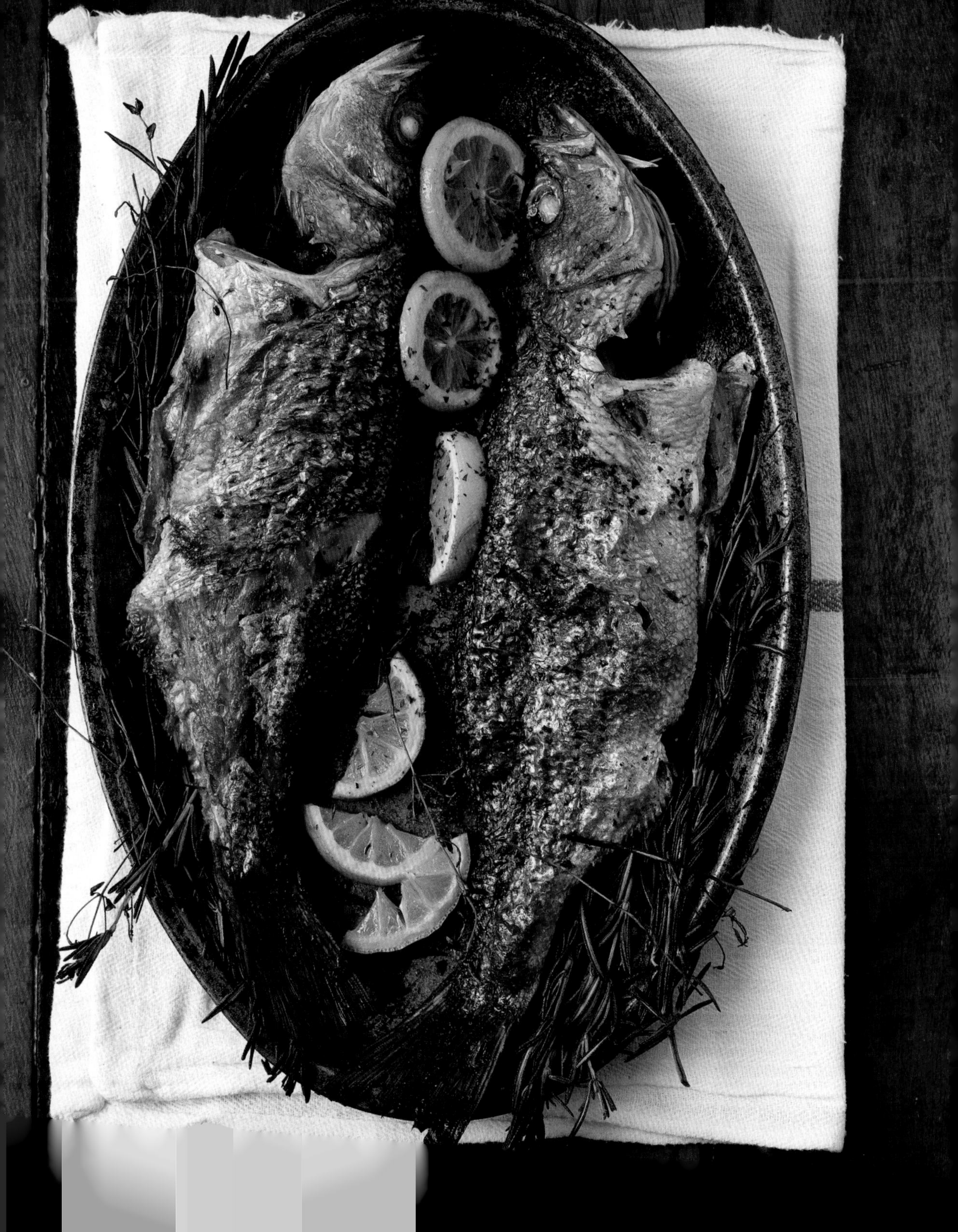

MARGHERITA PIZZA

CAVATELLI WITH PANCETTA
AND AVOCADO

PEAR AND PROSCIUTTO SALAD WITH
PORT GLAZE AND HERBED WALNUTS

THE ORCHARD SALAD

SKIRT STEAK WITH FLASH-SAUTÉED TOMATO AND BUFFALO MOZZARELLA SALAD

SALMON TARTARE WITH POTATO CRISPS AND RED ONION CRÈME FRAÎCHE

GNOCCHI WITH
HONEY-BRAISED SHORT RIBS

APPLE CRUMBLE

CREAMSICLE PANNA COTTA

ROASTED CHESTNUT SOUP

4 servings

This soup is a favorite at the Orchard, my newest restaurant, during the fall and winter months. I love the rich, earthy flavor of the roasted chestnuts. It smells great coming out of the kitchen—as soon as one of my waiters brings it to a table, more orders start coming in.

2 tablespoons butter

¼ cup chopped shallots

¼ cup peeled and diced potatoes (¼-inch dice)

2 teaspoons salt

½ teaspoon black pepper

I teaspoon chopped fresh thyme

4 cups roasted chestnuts (2½ to 3 pounds; see Note) or canned chestnuts in water, drained

7 cups Vegetable Stock (page 196)

½ cup heavy cream, plus extra for garnish

I tablespoon honey, plus extra for garnish

(Continued)

1. In a 2½-quart soup pot over low heat, combine the butter, shallots, potatoes, salt, pepper, and thyme. Cook until the potatoes soften and begin to brown, about 6 minutes. Raise the heat to medium, add 3½ cups of the chestnuts, and cook for 2 minutes, stirring frequently.

2. Add 6 cups of vegetable stock to the pot, increase the heat to high, and bring to a boil. Lower the heat to medium and simmer for 15 minutes, uncovered.

3. Set the soup aside to cool for a few minutes. Working in batches, pour the soup into a blender and blend until smooth, about 30 seconds for each batch. Pour extra stock in slowly if the soup is too thick.

4. Return the soup to the pot and stir in the cream and honey over medium heat. Taste to see if more salt is needed. Return the soup to a boil and cook for 2 minutes. Cut the remaining ½ cup of chestnuts into thin slices. To serve, divide the soup among 4 bowls. Place some of the sliced chestnuts in the center of each bow and drizzle with a little honey and cream.

Note: To roast chestnuts, slice an X on the flat side of each one with a paring knife. Brush a cookie sheet with 2 tablespoons of olive oil and lay the chestnuts on the sheet in one layer. Sprinkle with salt and pepper and roast at 400°F until tender, 15 to 20 minutes. Peel while still warm.

RED PEPPER AND FRESH BASIL SOUP WITH CRISPY SHALLOTS

4 servings

While the ingredients in this soup are classic Italian, this is an updated version of an old standby, which I remember having as a kid—about a million times. The crispy shallots give it a nice crunchy texture and a modern touch.

2 tablespoons butter

¼ cup diced shallots

1 teaspoon chopped garlic

3 red bell peppers, cut into ¼-inch dice (2½ to 3 cups)

¼ cup peeled and cubed potatoes (½-inch cubes)

½ cup chopped white button mushrooms (½-inch pieces)

2 teaspoons salt

½ teaspoon black pepper

2 tablespoons olive oil

1 tablespoon tomato paste

1½ teaspoons sugar

⅓ cup chopped fresh basil, plus extra for garnish

5 cups Vegetable Stock (page 196)

¼ cup heavy cream

Crispy Shallots (recipe follows)

(Continued)

1. In a 2½-quart soup pot over low heat, melt the butter with the shallots and garlic and cook until they begin to soften, about 3 minutes. Add the peppers, potatoes, mushrooms, salt, pepper, and olive oil. Cover the pot, raise the heat to medium, and cook until the vegetables begin to soften, about 5 minutes.

2. Add the tomato paste, sugar, and basil to the pot, and cook, stirring frequently, until the paste totally dissolves, 2 to 3 minutes. Add 4 cups of the vegetable stock, raise the heat to high, and bring the soup to a boil. Continue to cook, uncovered, for 10 minutes.

3. Set the soup aside to cool for a few minutes. Working in batches, pour the soup into a blender and blend until smooth, about 30 seconds for each batch. (At this point, the soup can be refrigerated for up to 2 days.)

4. Return the soup to the pot. Over medium heat, stir in the cream and more vegetable stock if the soup is too thick. Season with salt and pepper. Bring the soup to a boil and cook for 1 minute. Sprinkle a few crispy shallots and basil on top of the soup before serving.

CRISPY SHALLOTS

4 shallots, cut into thin rings (about 1 cup)
½ cup all-purpose flour
1 cup vegetable oil
1 teaspoon salt
Pinch of black pepper

1. Put the shallots in a medium mixing bowl. Sprinkle with the flour and toss gently with your hands. Carefully remove the shallots from the bowl, letting any excess flour fall off.

2. In a medium skillet, heat the oil until it is smoking. Using salad tongs, place the shallots in the oil and fry until golden brown, 6 to 7 minutes. Remove the shallots with the tongs and drain on paper towels. Sprinkle with salt and pepper. As the shallots cool, they will become crispy. The shallots can sit at room temperature until serving or stored for up to 1 day in an airtight container.

Eight

SALADS

CHERRY TOMATO, BACON, AND LEMON SALAD

4 servings

This salad has a lot of flavor, color, and texture. The lemon zest and juice add a bracing element, while the bacon's saltiness and crunch gives it a beautiful finish.

1 large lemon

1 tablespoon sugar

4 teaspoons extra-virgin olive oil

6 slices bacon, chopped into 1/4-inch pieces

2 cups halved yellow and red cherry tomatoes

1 tablespoon diced red onion

3 tablespoons torn fresh basil

1 tablespoon chopped fresh parsley

1/2 teaspoon salt

1/4 teaspoon black pepper

(Continued)

1. Using a zester or cheese grater, finely grate all the zest from the lemon. Try not to get any white pith with your zest. Set aside. Cut the lemon in half, squeeze the juice into a small bowl, and strain to remove all the seeds. Add the zest and sugar to the juice and mix well. Allow the mixture to stand for 15 minutes so the flavors can fully develop.

2. Heat 2 teaspoons of the olive oil in a medium skillet over medium heat until it begins to shimmer, 2 to 3 minutes. Add the bacon and cook until it begins to brown and crisp, about 5 minutes. Remove the bacon and drain on a paper towel.

3. In a medium mixing bowl, combine the tomatoes, onion, basil, parsley, salt, pepper, the remaining 2 teaspoons of olive oil, and lemon zest and juice. Divide the salad evenly among 4 salad plates. Sprinkle the bacon on top and serve.

ARUGULA AND
SOPPRESSATA SALAD

4 servings

If you like strong, spicy flavors, you'll love this salad. The bitterness of the arugula, the peppery soppressata, and the pickled capers dominate this dish. I serve this salad as part of an antipasto, but it's also great on crostini or even tossed with pasta and served cold.

4 cups baby arugula
2 celery stalks, cut into ½-inch pieces
1 small red onion, halved lengthwise and thinly sliced
1 cup halved yellow and red cherry tomatoes
1 cup pitted black olives, drained
4 ounces soppressata, thinly sliced
1 tablespoon capers, drained
⅓ cup extra-virgin olive oil
2 tablespoons red wine vinegar
1 teaspoon salt
Pinch of black pepper

1. In a large mixing bowl, combine the arugula, celery, onion, tomatoes, olives, soppressata, and capers.

2. Add the olive oil, vinegar, salt, and pepper, and toss well.

DRUNKEN GOAT CHEESE SALAD WITH CROUTONS AND CREAMY RED WINE VINAIGRETTE

4 servings

I fell in love with the flavor of drunken goat cheese and decided to build a salad around it. This Spanish cheese has a dark red rind, which is flavored with red wine, and is meant to be eaten. I buy it at Whole Foods or Dean & Deluca, but you can probably find it at any specialty cheese shop. The creamy red wine vinaigrette complements the flavors of both the cheese and rind, but the tastes are totally different.

For the croutons:

½ loaf crusty Italian bread, or 6 slices white bread (day-old is best)

2 tablespoons olive oil

½ teaspoon salt

Pinch of black pepper

1 teaspoon chopped fresh parsley

For the drunken goat cheese salad:

4 cups chopped romaine hearts (1-inch pieces)

1½ cups halved yellow and red cherry tomatoes

2 to 3 tablespoons Creamy Red Wine Vinaigrette (page 194)

6 ounces drunken goat cheese, cut into 1-inch wedges (about 12 wedges)

1. To make the croutons, remove the crusts from the bread and slice into 1-inch cubes. Heat the olive oil in a medium sauté pan over medium heat until it begins to smoke. Add the bread and fry, tossing frequently, until crispy, 7 to 10 minutes. Sprinkle with the salt, pepper, and parsley. Remove from the heat and set aside. (The cooled croutons can be stored in an airtight container at room temperature for 2 to 3 days.)

2. To make the salad, in a large mixing bowl, toss the romaine with the tomatoes and croutons. Drizzle with the creamy red wine vinaigrette and mix well.

3. Put 3 wedges of goat cheese on the edge of each salad plate. Place a mound of salad in the middle of the plate and serve.

THE ORCHARD SALAD

4 servings

This is a simple, quick, no-fuss salad that will make you look like you know what you're doing in the kitchen. It's on the sweet side and very light, which makes it great to serve with grilled meat.

For the salad:

 2 Granny Smith apples, cored

 ½ teaspoon fresh lemon juice

 5 cups roughly chopped red leaf lettuce

 ½ cup golden raisins

 1 cup halved herbed walnuts (page 134)

For the apple vinaigrette:

 ½ cup extra-virgin olive oil

 ¼ cup cider vinegar

 2 teaspoons chopped shallots

 1 tablespoon sugar

 2 teaspoons salt

 2 teaspoons fresh lemon juice

 2 teaspoons Dijon mustard

 ½ teaspoon black pepper

1. To make the salad, cut the apples into ¼-inch slices. Sprinkle with the lemon juice to keep them from turning brown. Set aside. In a large mixing bowl, combine the lettuce, raisins, and walnuts.

2. Put all the apple vinaigrette ingredients in a blender and blend for 20 seconds. (The vinaigrette can be stored in the refrigerator for up to 3 days.)

3. Pour ¼ cup of the apple vinaigrette into the mixing bowl and toss well to coat the lettuce.

4. Put a mound of salad in the center of each of 4 salad plates. Surround each mound with 4 to 6 apple slices, and serve.

PEAR AND PROSCIUTTO SALAD WITH PORT GLAZE AND HERBED WALNUTS

4 servings

This is one of the most popular appetizers at Ápizz, and one of my favorites, too. The integrity of the dish relies solely on the quality of the pears. Make sure they are on the softer side and remember that overripe is better than underripe. The sweet-salty-savory combination makes for interesting flavors, and the crispy prosciutto is an unexpected element.

1 tablespoon butter

2 tablespoons olive oil

1 sprig rosemary

3 to 4 sprigs thyme

½ cup walnut halves

½ teaspoon salt

4 Bartlett pears, cored and cut lengthwise into ½-inch wedges

4 ounces prosciutto, thinly sliced (12 to 15 slices)

8 ounces Parmigiano-Reggiano cheese, roughly chopped

For the port glaze:

⅓ cup tawny port wine

¼ cup balsamic vinegar

2 tablespoons plus 2 teaspoons sugar

1. Preheat the oven to 300°F. Melt the butter in a small sauté pan over low heat and add 1 tablespoon of the olive oil, the rosemary, and thyme. Cook for 5 minutes, so the flavors blend.

2. In a small mixing bowl, combine the herbs, walnuts, and salt. Mix to coat the nuts well.

3. Place the walnuts in a single layer on a baking sheet and bake for 15 minutes. Remove from the oven and allow the walnuts to cool to room temperature.

4. Heat the remaining 1 tablespoon of olive oil in a large sauté pan over medium heat until it begins to smoke. Add the prosciutto slices and cook for 4 to 5 minutes, turning them over frequently, until they are stiff and slightly crisp. Remove the prosciutto from the pan and drain on a paper towel.

5. To make the glaze, in a small saucepan over medium-high heat, combine the port wine, balsamic vinegar, and 2 tablespoons of the sugar and cook until the mixture reduces by half and turns syrupy, 10 to 12 minutes. Remove from the heat and stir in the remaining 2 teaspoons of sugar. Allow the glaze to cool to room temperature.

6. To assemble the dish, divide the pear slices among 4 plates, spacing them about 1 inch apart. Lay the prosciutto slices between the pears. Drizzle about 1 teaspoon of port glaze over each serving, and place a small mound of walnuts and Parmigiano-Reggiano on the side of each plate.

MIXED GREENS WITH FENNEL, ORANGE, AND PINK GRAPEFRUIT

4 servings

I love the combination of fennel and oranges. The pink grapefruit—one of my favorite fruits—really makes this salad jump. I make it for lunch when we go to Fire Island during the summer months. It will always remind me of the beach.

4 medium fennel bulbs, stalks cut off

I pink grapefruit

2 navel oranges

2 teaspoons sugar

⅓ cup vegetable oil

I teaspoon salt

¼ teaspoon black pepper

I tablespoon chopped fresh cilantro

2 cups mâche or other baby greens

2 cups frisée

I. Cut the fennel bulbs in quarters lengthwise. Cut into paper-thin slices with a mandolin or very sharp knife. Set aside.

2. Using a sharp knife, remove the peel and white pith from the grapefruit and oranges. Working over a bowl to catch the juice and using a small sharp knife, cut between the membranes of the grapefruit and oranges to release the segments, and cut the segments in half. Strain the juice and measure out ⅓ cup.

3. In a medium mixing bowl, whisk together the ⅓ cup of juice, and the sugar, oil, salt, pepper, and cilantro.

4. Combine the mâche and frisée in a large salad bowl. Pour the dressing over the greens and toss well. Add the fruit segments and fennel, toss gently, and serve.

Nine

PASTA & RISOTTO

OPEN RAVIOLI WITH ROASTED BUTTERNUT SQUASH

4 servings

This recipe came about out of necessity. I really wanted to offer a ravioli dish at Ápizz but was limited by the oven—typical ravioli need to be dropped into boiling water right before serving, a difficult step to do in a wood-burning oven. In this open version, the pasta can be preboiled, allowing us to cook the filling in the oven.

For the squash:

2 medium butternut squash, peeled and cut into ½-inch cubes

1 tablespoon salt

1 teaspoon freshly ground black pepper

½ cup brown sugar plus extra for sprinkling

1 stick butter

4 sheets pasta, 6 x 10 inches, or 4 extra-wide lasagna noodles

(Continued)

For the filling:

1½ cups ricotta cheese

½ cup mascarpone cheese

1 cup grated Parmigiano-Reggiano or domestic Parmesan cheese

Salt and black pepper to taste

3 tablespoons chopped fresh sage leaves

2 tablespoons chopped fresh parsley

2½ to 3 tablespoons butter

1. Preheat the oven to 375°F. To prepare the squash, in a large mixing bowl, combine the squash, salt, pepper, and brown sugar and mix gently.

2. In a medium saucepan over medium heat, melt the butter until it is completely liquefied. Pour the melted butter over the squash mixture and stir to combine. Spread out the squash mixture evenly on a baking sheet and roast for 25 to 30 minutes, or until the squash is tender.

3. Remove from the oven, sprinkle the squash lightly with additional brown sugar, and set aside.

4. To cook the pasta, bring a large pot of salted water to a boil. Add the pasta sheets and cook until almost al dente, but not quite.

5. Drain the pasta, place it on a work surface, and cut each sheet into quarters.

6. To make the filling, in a large bowl, combine the ricotta, mascarpone, Parmigiano-Reggiano, salt, and pepper and mix well until creamy. Mound 2 to 2½ tablespoons of the cheese mixture in the center of 8 of the pasta squares (you can use more cheese if you want cheesier ravioli).

7. Top each mound of cheese with another pasta square to form a sandwich (do not compress).

8. Butter a large ovenproof baking dish, and transfer the ravioli to the dish, leaving a small amount of space between them.

9. Top each square with about 1 teaspoon of butter and a teaspoon of chopped sage. Put an equal portion of the prepared squash mixture on top of each open ravioli and sprinkle with half of the chopped parsley.

10. Bake the ravioli and squash for 5 to 10 minutes, or until the butter melts and the cheese starts to bubble. Transfer the ravioli to a serving dish and garnish with the remaining chopped parsley.

PENNE WITH PARMIGIANO-REGGIANO AND ARUGULA

4 servings

This is a really simple pasta that screams "summer." The greens and the fresh flavors make it taste like a salad with the heartiness of a pasta dish.

1 pound penne pasta

3 tablespoons olive oil

2 tablespoons butter, at room temperature

½ cup grated Parmigiano-Reggiano plus one 3-ounce block

1 teaspoon salt

Black pepper to taste

½ cup roughly chopped fresh parsley

1 cup roughly chopped baby arugula

1 tablespoon fresh lemon juice

1. Cook the pasta in a large pot of boiling salted water until just tender but still firm. Drain the pasta, reserving ¼ cup of the cooking water.

2. In a large bowl, combine the drained pasta, olive oil, butter, and reserved pasta water, and stir until the butter melts. Add the grated cheese, salt, and pepper and toss well. Add the parsley, arugula, and lemon juice and toss well again. Shave the block of Parmigiano into paper-thin slices with a vegetable peeler or knife.

3. Divide the pasta among 4 plates. Top with the shaved Parmigiano slices and serve.

BUCATINI ALL'AMATRICIANA

4 servings

*Sometimes you just feel like having a plate of traditional pasta.
This recipe is simple and delicious, and is a staple in our home.*

¼ cup olive oil

4 ounces pancetta or bacon, cut into slivers

1 tablespoon chopped garlic

3 pepperoncini or cherry peppers, seeded and diced

½ cup finely chopped onion

1 cup halved cherry tomatoes

1 cup canned crushed plum tomatoes

2 tablespoons balsamic vinegar

½ cup Vegetable Stock (page 196)

2 teaspoons tomato paste

¼ cup fresh chopped basil

1 pound bucatini or spaghetti

½ cup grated Pecorino Romano cheese

Salt and black pepper to taste

1. Heat the oil and pancetta in a medium sauté pan over medium heat and cook for 3 minutes. Add the garlic and pepperoncini and cook until the peppers soften, 3 to 4 minutes. Raise the heat to high and add the onion, cherry and plum tomatoes, balsamic vinegar, stock, and tomato paste and let the mixture simmer until it thickens, about 8 to 10 minutes. Toss in the basil and stir well.

2. While the sauce is simmering, cook the pasta in a large pot of boiling salted water until tender yet firm. Drain the pasta and return it to the same pot.

3. Pour the tomato sauce and cheese over the pasta and mix well. Season with salt and pepper and serve.

PAPPARDELLE WITH LOBSTER TAIL
IN TOMATO-CREAM SAUCE

4 servings

This is a rich, decadent recipe, perfect for special occasions. I prefer using the meat of the lobster tail as it's the most tender. Using a good-quality frozen lobster tail is a simpler way to go than cooking a live lobster, and there isn't any wasted lobster meat.

½ cup Vegetable Stock (page 196)

¾ cup diced shallots

2 tablespoons chopped garlic

4 tablespoons butter

Four 12-ounce frozen lobster tails, thawed

1 cup halved yellow and red cherry tomatoes

1 cup heavy cream

½ cup chopped fresh basil, plus extra for garnish

1 tablespoon salt

½ teaspoon black pepper

1 pound pappardelle pasta

½ cup grated Parmigiano-Reggiano

1. In a large sauté pan over medium-high heat, combine the stock, shallots, garlic, and butter and heat until the butter is completely melted. Add the lobster tails and sauté until the shells are bright red, 4 to 5 minutes. Cover the pan, reduce the heat to low, and simmer until the lobster is cooked through, about 6 minutes. Remove the pan from the heat. Using a slotted spoon, transfer the lobster to a work surface. Let the lobster cool for a few minutes before handling.

2. Meanwhile, add the tomatoes, cream, basil, salt and pepper to the sauté pan. Simmer over medium heat until the tomatoes soften and the sauce thickens, about 10 minutes.

3. Remove the lobster meat from the shell and cut each tail in half lengthwise. Chop 4 halves into ½ inch pieces, and keep the remaining 4 halves intact to top each plate. Return the chopped lobster to the pan for 1 minute, just long enough for it to heat up.

4. Cook the pasta in a large pot of boiling salted water until tender yet firm. Drain the pasta and return it to the pot. Pour the sauce over the pasta, add the cheese and toss well. Divide the pasta among 4 plates. Place 1 lobster tail half on top of each plate, sprinkle with basil, and serve.

CAVATELLI WITH PANCETTA AND AVOCADO

4 servings

Our customers usually order this for the first time out of curiosity, and it always becomes one of their favorites. It's hard to imagine what sautéed avocado will taste like, especially with pasta and pancetta. In this case, the soft avocado is a beautiful counterpoint to the crispy pancetta and cavatelli al dente.

1 pound cavatelli pasta

¼ cup olive oil

8 thin slices pancetta, cut into long slivers

1 tablespoon chopped garlic

One 28-ounce can crushed plum tomatoes

1½ cups diced yellow and red cherry tomatoes

1 tablespoon salt

½ teaspoon black pepper

½ cup Vegetable Stock (page 196)

2 avocados, peeled, pitted, and cut into ½-inch cubes

½ cup heavy cream

¼ cup chopped fresh basil

¼ cup chopped fresh parsley

¼ cup grated Pecorino Romano cheese

1. Fill a 6- to 8-quart pot with water, add salt, and bring to a rapid boil. Add the pasta and cook until tender yet firm, 10 to 12 minutes. Drain the water, leaving the pasta in the pot with about ½ cup of the cooking water.

2. While the pasta is cooking, heat the olive oil in a medium sauté pan over medium-high heat until it begins to shimmer. Add the pancetta and garlic and cook until the pancetta begins to brown and crisp, about 3 minutes. Add the plum and cherry tomatoes, salt, pepper, and stock, and cook until the tomatoes are very soft, about 5 minutes. Add the avocados and cream and bring to a boil. Lower the heat, add the basil, parsley, and cheese, and cook for another 2 minutes. Add the sauce to the pasta pot and stir gently. Serve on warm plates.

BASIC RISOTTO

4 servings

*At Ápizz, we serve risotto as a main course as well as on the side with meat or fish.
I always start my risotto with this recipe—it's a great base for
playing around with different seasonal toppings.*

2 tablespoons olive oil

½ cup chopped onions

I teaspoon salt

2 cups Carnaroli or Arborio rice

½ cup dry white wine

2 to 3 cups Vegetable Stock (page 196)

1. Heat the oil, onions, and salt in a medium sauté pan over medium heat and cook until the onions soften, about 5 minutes.

2. Add the rice and stir well until coated with oil and the onions are thoroughly mixed in. When the mixture starts to get a little dry, add the white wine and stir until the smell of alcohol is gone, about 5 minutes. Stir in the stock, 1 cup at a time, until the rice is about half cooked. Be sure to allow each cup to be absorbed before adding the next and stir often, 8 to 10 minutes.

3. At this point, you can add any of the purees and vegetables found in my risotto recipes to finish the dish, or flavor the risotto with your own seasonings.

LEEK AND PEA RISOTTO

4 servings

This is a perfect spring dish, and I try to put it on the menu as soon as the peas hit the Greenmarket. At Ápizz, we serve it as a main course, but at home we often pair it with grilled fish.

For the leek puree:

2 tablespoons olive oil

1 tablespoon diced shallots

¼ cup peeled and diced potato

1 cup chopped leeks (white and light green parts)

1 teaspoon salt

Pinch of black pepper

For the sliced leeks and peas:

½ cup olive oil

2 tablespoon butter

3 tablespoons diced shallots

2 teaspoons chopped garlic

2 cups shelled English peas (about 2 pounds in their shells)

3 cups slivered leeks (cut lengthwise, white and pale green parts only)

1 tablespoon salt

Pinch of black pepper

2 cups Vegetable Stock (page 196)

2 tablespoons chopped fresh basil

2 tablespoons chopped fresh parsley

1 tablespoon chopped fresh thyme

1 recipe Basic Risotto (page 146)

(Continued)

1. To prepare the puree, in a medium sauté pan over medium heat, combine the olive oil, shallots, and potatoes. Cook until the shallots are soft and the potatoes begin to brown, 3 to 5 minutes. Add the leeks, salt, and pepper and cook until the leeks soften and wilt, about 5 minutes.

2. Add enough water to cover the leeks and simmer until they are very soft, about 10 minutes. Strain the mixture until all the liquid is removed. Set the liquid aside for blending.

3. Put the leek mixture in a blender and add just enough of the strained liquid to cover. Puree the leeks until they are smooth, adding more liquid if it's too thick. (Consistency should be like cake batter.)

4. To prepare the sliced leeks and peas, heat the olive oil and butter in a large sauté pan over medium heat until the butter melts. Add the shallots and garlic and cook for 2 minutes. Add the peas, leeks, salt, and pepper and cook for 4 to 5 minutes. Add the stock, basil, parsley, and thyme and cook until the peas and leeks are tender, 10 to 12 minutes. Remove the vegetables with a slotted spoon, and discard the liquid.

5. Combine the puree with the basic risotto recipe on page 000. Mix half the vegetables with the risotto. Divide the risotto among 4 dinner plates. Scatter a quarter of the remaining vegetables on top of each plate. Serve immediately.

MUSHROOM RISOTTO

4 servings

I wanted to do a great mushroom risotto at Ápizz, but it took me a while to get it just right. When I first started experimenting with the dish, I was using the Basic Risotto recipe on page 146 and mixing in a variety of sautéed mushrooms. But that rich, earthy flavor I was going for just wasn't in every bite. One day, I threw some mushrooms in the blender along with some shallots and a little potato as a thickener. The result was delicious—a rich and very flavorful puree that was good enough to eat right out of the blender with a spoon. I mixed it into the risotto and everything fell into place.

For the mushroom puree:

¼ cup olive oil

¼ cup chopped shallots

½ potato, peeled and diced

2 cups chopped cremini mushrooms

Salt and black pepper to taste

For the mushroom topping:

⅛ cup olive oil

1½ shallots, chopped

1 clove garlic, chopped

2 cups cremini mushrooms, cleaned and cut in half

Salt and pepper

½ tablespoon thyme

1 recipe Basic Risotto (page 146)

(Continued)

1. To prepare the puree, heat the olive oil in a small sauté pan over medium heat until it begins to shimmer. Add the shallots and cook until they begin to brown, about 3 minutes. Add the potatoes and cook until they soften and begin to brown, 8 to 10 minutes. Add the mushrooms, salt, and pepper, and just enough water to cover the mixture. Cook over medium heat until the liquid reduces by half, about 10 minutes.

2. Remove the mushroom mixture from the heat, pour into a blender and puree until smooth, about 30 seconds. Keeps in refrigerator for 2 to 3 days.

3. To prepare the mushroom topping, heat the olive oil in a medium sauté pan over medium heat until it begins to shimmer, about 1 or 2 minutes. Add the shallots and garlic and brown slightly, about 2 or 3 minutes. Add the mushrooms, salt, pepper, and thyme and cook until the mushrooms are soft, about 5 minutes.

4. Combine the puree with the basic risotto recipe. Mix half the mushrooms into the risotto and divide evenly among 4 plates. Top with the remaining mushrooms.

GNOCCHI

4 servings

This is a basic gnocchi recipe that can be served with a simple tomato sauce or something more complicated. At Ápizz we have served it with everything from a fresh pesto to a heartier braised short rib ragù.

3 baking potatoes (1½ to 1¾ pounds)

1 egg

¾ cup grated Parmigiano-Reggiano cheese

2 tablespoons salt

1 teaspoon black pepper

¼ cup chopped fresh basil

2 cups all-purpose flour plus extra for dusting

1. Preheat the oven to 375°F. Prick the potatoes with a fork, wrap in aluminum foil and bake them for 50 minutes or until tender. Remove the aluminum foil and set the potatoes aside to cool for a few minutes before handling. Scrape the skins from the potatoes with a paring knife. Press the potatoes through a potato ricer or grate on a cheese grater. Spread out the potatoes in a thin, even layer on a work surface. Let them cool completely.

2. In a medium mixing bowl, whisk together the egg, Parmesan, salt, pepper, and basil. Gather the potatoes into a mound and form a well in the center. Pour the egg mixture into the well. Knead the potato and egg mixture together, gradually adding enough of the flour, about 1½ cups, to form a slightly sticky yet smooth dough.

(Continued)

3. Use some of the remaining ½ cup of flour to dust the dough, your hands, and the work surface. Cut a piece of the dough small enough to fit in the palm of your hand. Using the palms of your hands, roll the cut piece into a long cigar shape, about ½ inch in diameter. Put the piece back on the work surface and cut into 1-inch-long pieces. Using your index finger and thumb, gently pinch the sides together to form an indent. Repeat the process with the rest of the dough. The gnocchi can be set aside at room temperature for up to 30 minutes or stored in the refrigerator for 1 hour before cooking. Or you can freeze them (see Note).

4. In a large pot over high heat, bring 6 quarts of salted water to a rapid boil. Drop about half the gnocchi into the boiling water, a few at a time. Once the gnocchi rise to the surface of the water, cook for 1 more minute before removing with a slotted spoon. Cook the remaining gnocchi. Top the gnocchi with one of the sauce recipes that follow.

Note: I recommend freezing the gnocchi uncooked. Once you have formed them into the dumpling shape (step 3), arrange them in a single layer in a baking pan. Place the pan in the freezer and freeze for about 3 to 4 hours. Put the frozen gnocchi in a freezer bag and store them for up to 6 weeks.

GNOCCHI WITH
HONEY-BRAISED SHORT RIBS

6 to 8 servings

This is a really hearty, stick-to-your-ribs kind of dish, and a big seller on cold winter nights. The honey imparts a subtle sweetness to the meat, which is a perfect counterpart to the potato gnocchi—call it my version of meat and potatoes.

6 short ribs (8 to 10 pounds)

Salt and black pepper to taste

Flour for dusting

¼ cup olive oil (more if needed)

2 onions, diced

2 carrots, peeled and diced

3 celery stalks, diced

2 cups red wine

Two 28-ounce cans crushed tomatoes

1 cup honey

2 sprigs fresh thyme

1 recipe Gnocchi (page 151)

Grated Parmigiano-Reggiano for serving

(Continued)

1. Place the short ribs on a work surface. Sprinkle both sides generously with salt and pepper. Dust the short ribs with enough flour to cover both sides.

2. Heat the olive oil in a large stockpot over medium heat until it begins to smoke. Add the ribs one at a time (be careful as the oil will spatter). Brown them evenly on all sides. Remove the ribs from the pot and set aside.

3. Combine the onion, carrots, celery, salt, and pepper in the stockpot used for browning the ribs. Cook the vegetables over medium heat until they are soft, 10 to 15 minutes, adding more oil if they become too dry. Add the wine and bring to a boil. Add the meat, tomatoes, ½ cup of the honey, the thyme, and 2 cups of water and cover. Simmer until the meat is falling off the bone, 2 to 2½ hours.

4. Remove the meat from the pot and set aside to cool before handling. Using your hands, shred the meat, removing any bone and large pieces of fat.

5. Strain the sauce into a large bowl and discard the vegetables and thyme. Stir the remaining ½ cup of honey into the sauce and add the meat. To serve, spoon the meat sauce over the gnocchi and sprinkle with Parmesan cheese.

GNOCCHI WITH TOMATO, BLACK OLIVE, AND BASIL SAUCE

4 servings

This dish was a work in progress. It began as a simple plate of gnocchi with tomato sauce and fresh basil, and it was delicious. But then I craved a more intense flavor so I started playing around with black olives, first tossing them into the dish at the last minute, and later sautéing them in butter. The latter worked beautifully, and really gave the sauce a subtle pungency.

2 tablespoons butter
½ cup pitted and halved black olives
2 cups Basic Tomato Sauce (page 197)
½ cup chopped fresh basil, plus extra for garnish
Pinch of salt
Pinch of black pepper
Gnocchi (page 151)
½ cup grated Parmigiano-Reggiano cheese

1. In a medium sauté pan over medium heat, melt the butter until it foams. Add the black olives and cook for 2 minutes. Add the tomato sauce and bring to a simmer. Add the basil, salt, and pepper and cook for 2 more minutes. Remove the pan from the heat and set aside.

2. In a large pot over high heat, bring 6 quarts of salted water to a rapid boil. Drop about half the gnocchi into the boiling water, a few at a time. Once the gnocchi rise to the surface, cook for 1 more minute before removing with a slotted spoon. Continue with remaining gnocchi.

3. Return the tomato sauce to a simmer over low heat. Add the gnocchi and stir gently until well coated. Stir in the grated cheese. Divide the gnocchi among 4 plates. Top with a sprinkling of basil and serve.

RIGATONI WITH SWEET ITALIAN SAUSAGE AND TOMATO CREAM SAUCE

4 servings

This hearty pasta is one of our mainstays for staff meals. The only question about this dish is whether to use sweet or spicy sausage. The Spanish guys in our kitchen love it as hot as humanly possible, but we tone it down for the waitstaff.

1 pound rigatoni

3 tablespoons olive oil

1 pound sweet Italian sausages, casings removed, and crumbled

½ teaspoon crushed red pepper

¾ cup diced shallots

¼ cup chopped garlic

1 tablespoon tomato paste

1 cup Vegetable Stock (page 196)

One 28-ounce can whole plum tomatoes, drained and roughly chopped

½ cup halved cherry tomatoes

2 teaspoons salt

Pinch of black pepper

½ cup heavy cream

½ cup loosely packed fresh basil, cut into slivers plus extra for garnish

½ cup grated Parmigiano-Reggiano

Crusty Italian bread for serving

1. Cook the pasta in a large pot of boiling salted water until tender yet firm.

2. While the pasta is cooking, start preparing the sauce: Heat the oil in a large, heavy sauté pan over medium-high heat until it begins to shimmer, 1 or 2 minutes. Add the sausage and red pepper, breaking the sausage up with the back of a fork, and sauté until the sausage is no longer pink, about 4 minutes. Add the shallots, garlic, and tomato paste and ½ cup of stock and cook until the sausage begins to brown, about 4 minutes. Add the rest of the stock, the plum and cherry tomatoes, salt, and pepper and cook until the sauce starts to thicken, 6 to 8 minutes. Add the cream and simmer for another 2 minutes. Stir in the basil and remove from the heat.

3. Drain the pasta and return it to the same pot. Add the sauce and mix well over medium-low heat for 2 minutes. Divide the pasta among 4 bowls. Sprinkle basil and Parmigiano-Reggiano over the top of each plate. Serve with lots of crusty Italian bread.

LASAGNA WITH BRAISED
SHORT RIBS

10 servings

I wanted to serve lasagna at Ápizz because I knew it would work well in our wood-
burning oven. But I didn't want to serve the same old lasagna that I grew up
eating and that you can get anywhere in Little Italy. I decided to replace the
traditional ground beef with braised wild boar, which has a completely
different consistency from chopped meat. It was a hit and
remains one of our most popular dishes.

*Since wild boar can be hard to come by, I've replaced it here with short ribs, which,
when braised, have a similar consistency. You can prepare the sauce and the
ribs a day or two ahead of time and store, covered, in the refrigerator.*

⅔ cup olive oil

6 pounds short ribs, cut in half

Flour for dusting meat

1 cup diced carrot

1 cup diced celery

1 cup diced onion

Salt and black pepper to taste

2 cups red wine

Seven 28-ounce cans crushed tomatoes

1 bunch fresh thyme, separated

Butter for coating the pans

10 to 12 lasagna sheets (10 x 6 inches), boiled until al dente

3 to 4 cups grated Parmigiano-Reggiano cheese

½ cup chopped fresh parsley

1. Heat the oil in a large stockpot over medium heat until it begins to smoke. Meanwhile, dust both sides of the short ribs with flour. Add the short ribs to the pot in one layer (if there's not enough room in the pot, work in batches) and cook until all sides are browned evenly. Remove the ribs from the pot and set aside.

2. Add the carrots, celery, onion, salt, and pepper to the stockpot. Cook the vegetables over medium heat until they are soft, 10 to 15 minutes, adding more oil if they become too dry. Add the red wine and simmer, covered, until the alcohol smell disappears, 5 to 10 minutes. Add the crushed tomatoes, thyme, and salt to taste and stir well. Put the meat back in the pot and cover. Bring to a boil, then lower heat. Simmer until the meat is falling off the bone, 2 to 2½ hours.

3. Remove the meat from the pot and set aside to cool before handling. Using your hands, shred the meat, removing any bone and large pieces of fat. Set the meat aside. Strain the sauce into a bowl and discard the vegetables and thyme.

4. To assemble the lasagna: Preheat the oven to 350°F. You will need either one very large pan, about 20 x 12 x 3 inches, or 2 smaller pans. Grease the bottom of the pan with butter. Line the bottom of the pan with pasta sheets, allowing them to overlap. Scatter one layer of meat over the pasta until it is nearly covered. Do not pack the meat down. Spoon some sauce over the meat, then sprinkle with some grated cheese. Cover with a second layer of pasta and repeat the process. End with a layer of pasta with a generous sprinkling of cheese over it. Cover the pan with aluminum foil and bake for 35 to 40 minutes, until the cheese is melted and the pasta is lightly browned on top. Allow the lasagna to rest for 15 to 20 minutes before serving. Serve with extra sauce and grated cheese on the side and garnish each serving with chopped parsley.

SWEET POTATO AGNOLOTTI WITH CHESTNUT CREAM SAUCE

4 to 6 servings

I always like to have one sweet pasta dish on my menus. It's a nice contrast to the red and garlicky sauces I tend to work with. This one was on the very first menu I designed for the Orchard. Since we opened the restaurant in November, I wanted to work with fall ingredients, but use them in an unexpected way.

For the agnolotti dough:

   1¾ cups all-purpose flour, plus extra for dusting

   6 egg yolks plus 1 whole egg

   1½ tablespoons olive oil

   1 tablespoon milk

For the sweet potato filling:

   2 pounds sweet potatoes, peeled and cut into ½-inch cubes

   4 tablespoons chopped fresh sage

   1 teaspoon ground cinnamon

   ½ teaspoon ground nutmeg

   6 tablespoons butter, at room temperature

   ¼ cup lightly packed brown sugar

For the chestnut cream sauce:

   Two 10-ounce cans whole chestnuts packed in water

   6 tablespoons butter

   ½ cup chopped shallots

   1 cup diced potatoes

   10 to 15 sprigs fresh thyme

   2 to 3 cups Vegetable Stock (page 196)

   1 tablespoon honey

   1 teaspoon plus pinch of salt

   ⅓ cup heavy cream

2 tablespoons chopped fresh sage

Pinch of grated Parmigiano-Reggiano cheese

Pinch of black pepper

1. To make the dough: Pour the flour onto a work surface in one large mound. Using two fingers, stir a well about 8 inches in diameter and 2 inches high in the center of the mound. In a small mixing bowl, combine the egg yolks, whole egg, olive oil, and milk. Pour the mixture into the center of the well. Using two fingers, gently stir the mixture around, slowly brushing against the inner wall of the flour and bringing flour into the well. Continue to expand the well until all the flour is combined with the egg mixture.

2. With both hands, knead the mixture into one large ball. Press the ball with the heels of your hands and knead it back into a ball. Continue pressing and kneading for 12 to 15 minutes, until the ball becomes harder and firmer and takes on a doughy consistency. Wrap the dough in plastic wrap and allow it to rest at room temperature for 30 minutes.

3. To make the filling: Fill a medium pot three-quarters full of water. Add the sweet potatoes and bring the water to a boil over high heat. Cook the potatoes until they are soft, 20 to 25 minutes.

4. In the meantime, blanch the sage by submerging it in a small pot of boiling water for 2 to 3 minutes. Remove the pot from the heat and drain the water. Set the sage aside.

5. Remove the potatoes from the heat and drain. With a whisk or potato masher, break up the potatoes until almost completely mashed. Add the cinnamon and nutmeg and mix well.

6. In a medium sauté pan over medium heat, melt the butter with the brown sugar until the sugar is fully dissolved, about 4 minutes. Remove from the heat, add the mixture to the potatoes, and mix well. Set aside.

7. To make the sauce: Drain the chestnuts and roughly chop them. Set them aside. In a large sauté pan over medium heat, melt the butter until it begins to foam. Add the shallots and diced potatoes and cook until they soften and are slightly brown, 5 to 7 minutes. Add the chestnuts

(Continued)

and thyme to the pan and mix well. Add enough stock to cover the mixture completely and cook until the stock is reduced by half, about 15 minutes. Remove the pan from the heat.

8. Remove the thyme from the pan and discard. Pour the mixture into a food processor or blender and blend until it is completely smooth, 30 seconds to 1 minute. Add ½ cup of vegetable stock and blend for an additional 10 seconds. Pour the mixture into a bowl and whisk in the honey and 1 teaspoon of salt.

9. Scrape the brown bits from the bottom of the sauté pan to flavor the sauce. Pour the mixture back into the pan and heat over medium heat. Add the cream, sage, cheese, pinch of salt, and black pepper and stir well. Reduce the heat to low and simmer the sauce while you make the agnolotti.

10. To make the pasta sheets: Dust a work surface with flour. Cut the ball of dough in half and work with one half at a time. Divide the half into 2 or 3 pieces. Run each piece through a pasta machine to make sheets that are 5 to 6 inches wide. The sheets should be thin, but not translucent. Repeat the process with the remaining dough.

11. To fill the agnolotti: Lay the pasta sheets on a lightly floured surface. Using a sharp knife, trim the edges so they are even and straight. Place the potato filling in a pastry bag with a plain round tip and squeeze out a line of filling across the bottom of the pasta sheet. Be sure to leave a ¾-inch border along the bottom, left, and right edges. Carefully pull the bottom edge of the pasta up and over the filling and seal the agnolotti by pressing gently with your finger. Next, seal the left and right edges of the agnolotti.

12. Use your fingers to gently pinch the pasta in 1-inch increments, leaving about ¾ inch of space between the agnolotti. Trim the top edge of the dough, detaching the filled agnolotti from the remainder of the pasta sheet. Be careful not to cut too close to the filling, or you will break the seal. Separate the agnolotti from one another by cutting the center of each pinched section. Set aside the finished agnolotti on a work surface or baking sheet pan dusted with flour, and make the rest of the agnolotti.

13. Drop the agnolotti in a large pot of boiling salted water and cook for 5 to 7 minutes. Cook in batches, if necessary. Remove with a slotted spoon, and arrange on dinner plates. Spoon the sauce over the agnolotti and serve immediately.

FARFALLE WITH GREEN BEANS, POTATOES, AND PESTO

4 to 6 servings

This is one of my wife's favorite recipes, so I cook it a lot at home. The green beans make it a great springtime dish, and the potatoes, while subtle, add a really nice texture to the pasta.

3 cups fresh basil leaves

1½ cups olive oil

⅓ cup pine nuts

¼ cup walnut halves

1 cup grated Parmigiano-Reggiano cheese plus extra for garnish

2 teaspoons chopped garlic

10 ounces green beans, trimmed and cut in half

1 medium baking potato, peeled and cut into ½-inch cubes

1 pound farfalle pasta

Salt and black pepper to taste

(Continued)

1. Combine the basil, ¾ cup of the olive oil, the pine nuts, walnuts, cheese, and garlic in a blender and blend until smooth, about 1 minute. With the blender running, gradually add the remaining ¾ cup oil. Pour the mixture into a bowl and set aside.

2. Cook the green beans in a large pot of boiling salted water until they are tender yet firm, about 5 minutes. Remove the beans with a strainer and put them in a bowl. Return the cooking water to a boil. Add the potatoes and cook until tender, about 7 minutes. Remove the potatoes with a strainer and add to the beans. Return the cooking water to a boil and add the farfalle. Cook the pasta until it is tender yet firm, 8 to 10 minutes. Drain the pasta, reserving 1 cup of the cooking water. Return the green beans, potatoes, and pasta to the pot. Add the pesto and toss well to coat. Gradually add enough reserved water to coat the pasta with a moist sauce. Season with salt and pepper, and add more cheese if desired.

Ten

MEATS & POULTRY

BALSAMIC-GLAZED PORK CHOPS
4 servings

*I have always loved pork chops with sweet flavors, whether the sweetness comes
from a side dish like sautéed lady apples or from a glaze, as it does here.
The balsamic vinegar, when cooked with sugar, turns into a beautiful sweet syrup,
a perfect contrast to the savory meat. At Ápizz we'll serve these caramelized
pork chops with a simple green salad in the summer and hearty
mashed sweet potatoes during the colder months.*

4 center-cut pork chops, ¾ inch thick

¼ cup olive oil plus extra to rub on chops

1 tablespoon salt

1 teaspoon black pepper

¼ cup diced shallots

1 tablespoon chopped fresh parsley

1 tablespoon chopped fresh thyme

1 teaspoon chopped fresh rosemary

1 cup aged balsamic vinegar from Modena

1 tablespoon brown sugar

(Continued)

1. Rub the pork chops with olive oil and sprinkle with salt and pepper.

2. Heat the oil in a 12-inch heavy skillet over medium-high heat until it's hot, but not smoking. Add the shallots to the pan and cook for 1 minute. Add the chops and cook for 4 to 5 minutes on one side, or until they're golden brown. Flip the chops over, sprinkle with the parsley, thyme, and rosemary, and cook until they are cooked through, 3 to 4 minutes. Transfer the chops to a plate and set aside.

3. Add the balsamic vinegar and sugar to the pan, raise the heat to high, and cook until the sauce thickens slightly, about 4 minutes. Reduce the heat to medium and return the chops to the pan along with any juices on the plate. Heat the chops and sauce for 2 to 3 minutes, turning the chops over midway through cooking. Place 1 chop on each dinner plate. Spoon some sauce over each chop and serve.

BRAISED CHICKEN AND POTATOES IN TOMATO SAUCE

6 servings

This is another favorite dish at staff meals. It's flavorful, straightforward, and versatile, and appeals to a wide range of picky eaters. At Ápizz, we make a big pot of rice so everyone can spoon the chicken and sauce on top.

Two 3 to 3½-pound chickens, cut into 8 pieces each

2 tablespoons salt

2 teaspoons black pepper

½ cup olive oil

2 cups peeled and cubed potatoes (½-inch cubes)

1 large onion, chopped

1 red bell pepper, chopped

1 yellow bell pepper, chopped

2 tablespoons tomato paste

¼ cup chopped fresh basil

¼ cup chopped garlic

1 cup red wine

Two 28-ounce cans whole tomatoes in juice

1 cup Vegetable Stock (page 196)

(Continued)

1. Pat the chickens dry and sprinkle all sides with 1 tablespoon of the salt and 1 teaspoon of the pepper. Set aside.

2. In a heavy pan 14 inches in diameter and 3 to 4 inches deep, heat ¼ cup of the olive oil over high heat until it is hot but not smoking. Place 8 pieces of chicken in the pan and brown evenly on both sides, about 5 minutes on each side. Transfer the chicken to a plate, pour the oil out of the pan and wipe out lightly with a paper towel, leaving behind a residue of oil. Cook the remaining chicken in the remaining ¼ cup of oil and transfer the chicken to a plate, but leave the oil in the pan.

3. Add the potatoes to the pan and cook over high heat until they begin to brown, 3 to 4 minutes. Reduce the heat to medium and add the onion, peppers, tomato paste, basil, garlic, and the remaining tablespoon of salt and teaspoon of pepper. Cook, stirring occasionally and scraping up any browned bits, until the onion and garlic are slightly brown and the peppers begin to soften, 8 to 10 minutes. Add the wine and simmer for 2 to 3 minutes. Add the tomatoes with their juice and the stock and simmer, breaking up the tomatoes with a wooden spoon, for 5 minutes. Return the chicken to the pot, cover loosely, and simmer until the meat is cooked through and tender, about 35 to 40 minutes. Serve on individual plates or in one large casserole dish for family-style dining.

VEAL, BEEF, AND PORK MEATBALLS WITH RICOTTA FILLING

8 to 10 servings

Mmmmm, meatballs. I love meatballs, but the truth is that I never set out to stake my reputation on them. When I was growing up, meatballs were the thing that excited me most about Sunday dinner. I would eat one or two as soon as they were out of the frying pan. At dinner, I felt the pasta was more of garnish to the meatballs than anything else. That's why I wanted to make a meal out of them at Ápizz—two meatballs the size of your head served in a dish with sauce. No pasta, period.

When I started playing around with my recipe, I experimented with several variations of the meat: pork and veal, pork and beef, and veal alone, but the best version contained all three. The flavors were richer and more complex. As for frying versus baking, my choice to bake had nothing to do with a health issue. It was all about my wood-burning oven; it happens to turn out excellent meatballs.

For the meatballs:

3 cups cubed crustless *filone* or regular Italian bread (about ½ loaf)

1 pound ground veal

1 pound ground beef

1 pound ground pork

1 egg

½ onion, chopped

¼ cup chopped fresh parsley

¼ cup chopped fresh basil

1½ cups grated Parmigiano-Reggiano cheese

Pinch of oregano

Salt and black pepper to taste

2 cups Basic Tomato Sauce (page 197)

(Continued)

For the stuffing:
   1 cup ricotta cheese
   ½ cup grated Parmigiano-Reggiano cheese
   1½ teaspoons salt
   Black pepper to taste

To finish the meatballs:
   1 cup Basic Tomato Sauce (page 197)
   ½ cup ricotta cheese
   ¼ cup grated Parmigiano-Reggiano cheese

1. To make the meatballs, preheat the oven to 350°F. Run the cubed bread under water and gently squeeze out the excess liquid. Put the bread in a large mixing bowl. Add the remaining meatball ingredients to the bowl, except for the tomato sauce, and mix well with your hands. Divide the mixture into 8 equal portions. Using your hands, roll each portion into a large round meatball, about the size of an apple. Place the meatballs in a medium to large baking dish.

2. In a separate bowl, combine the tomato sauce and 2 cups water. Spoon the tomato sauce and water mixture over the meatballs until the liquid comes three-quarters of the way up (if more liquid is needed, add water). Cover the baking dish with aluminum foil and bake the meatballs for 1 hour, turning the dish after 30 minutes. Remove the baking dish from the oven, drain and discard the liquid, and let the meatballs cool to room temperature. (The meatballs can also be stored in the refrigerator for up to 3 days.)

3. To make the stuffing, in a medium mixing bowl, combine the ricotta cheese with the Parmigiano, salt, and pepper.

4. Using an apple corer or small knife, core out a hole to the bottom of the meatball that is about ½ inch in diameter. Fill the hole with the cheese mixture (for best results, use a pastry bag).

5. To finish, spoon the 1 cup of tomato sauce evenly over the meatballs and heat for 10 to 15 minutes at 350°F. Remove the pan from the oven. Place 1 tablespoon of ricotta cheese on top of each meatball (it should look like the cheese is oozing out of the center), sprinkle with Parmigiano cheese, and heat for an additional 3 minutes.

MINT ORZO WITH
SLICED LAMB TENDERLOIN

4 servings

Since I was a kid, I have always loved lamb with mint. I wanted to work with these flavors but wasn't about to use the mint jelly found in the classic version of this dish. The orzo recipe below introduces the taste of mint in an unexpected way.

For the lamb:

1 to 1½ pounds lamb tenderloin, trimmed of any fat

1 tablespoon olive oil

1 teaspoon salt

Pinch of black pepper

1 tablespoon chopped fresh thyme

For the orzo:

2 tablespoons olive oil

1 tablespoon butter

¼ cup diced shallots

2 teaspoons salt

Pinch of black pepper

2 cups orzo

¼ cup dry white wine

4 cups Vegetable Stock (page 196)

1 tablespoon crème fraîche

¼ cup chopped fresh mint

1 tablespoon chopped fresh parsley

Salt and black pepper to taste

(Continued)

1. To prepare the lamb, place the tenderloin between 2 sheets of plastic wrap on a work surface. Using a kitchen mallet, pound the lamb until it is about ¼ inch thick.

2. Rub the lamb with olive oil, covering both sides. Sprinkle salt, pepper, and thyme on both sides. Put the lamb in a large sauté pan over medium heat and cook for 2 to 3 minutes on each side. Remove the lamb from the pan and slice into ½-inch strips.

3. To prepare the orzo, heat the olive oil in a medium sauté pan over medium heat, until it is hot but not smoking. Add the butter, shallots, salt, and pepper to the pan and sauté until the shallots are soft, 4 to 5 minutes. Add the orzo, stirring constantly until it begins to toast and turn light brown, about 5 minutes. Add the wine and continue stirring until the alcohol smell is gone and the wine is completely absorbed, 3 to 4 minutes. Add 1½ cups of the vegetable stock, stirring constantly until it is absorbed. Add more stock, a little at a time, until the orzo is creamy and firm (you may not need to use all the stock). Add the crème fraîche, mint, parsley, salt, and pepper and mix well.

4. Divide the orzo among 4 dinner plates. Place the slices of lamb next to the orzo and serve.

ROASTED CORNISH HENS

4 servings

I love the juicy flavor of Cornish hens and was determined to put this dish on one of my menus. Since it would have looked like an oddball at Ápizz—it's as American as you can get—I serve it at the Orchard during the fall and winter months. A whole hen on a dinner plate always impresses diners—you can hear the "oohs" and "aahs" whenever it hits the table.

For the hens:

4 Rock Cornish hens, about 1½ pounds each

Salt and black pepper

24 sprigs fresh rosemary

24 sprigs fresh thyme

1 cup fresh basil leaves, lightly packed

½ cup fresh mint leaves, lightly packed

2 sticks butter

For the potatoes:

4 baking potatoes, peeled and cubed

1½ sticks butter

2 cups heavy cream

1 teaspoon white truffle oil

Salt and black pepper to taste

1. To roast the hens, preheat the oven to 375°F. Remove bags with the gizzards and liver from the cavities of the hens and set aside until you make the potatoes. Rinse the hens inside and out with cold water and pat dry. Remove any excess skin near the cavities with kitchen scissors or a knife. Generously sprinkle the hens inside and out with salt and pepper. Set aside.

2. Lay 4 separate rectangles of cheesecloth measuring about 10 x 12 inches on a flat surface. Trim 12 rosemary and 12 thyme sprigs to 4 inches in length. Combine the rosemary and

(Continued)

thyme with half of the basil and half of the mint. Put a quarter of the mixed herbs onto one end of each piece of cheesecloth. Roll the cloths like cigars, fold in the ends and secure the bundles with kitchen twine. Set aside. Use the remaining herbs to make a bed on a small to medium baking pan at least 1 inch deep. Place the hens on top of the bed of herbs.

3. Melt the butter in a small to medium saucepan over medium heat until it is slightly brown and nutty, 3 to 4 minutes. Spoon 2 teaspoons of the melted butter into each hen's cavity. Pour the remaining butter over the hens, using your fingers to rub the butter around and coat each hen evenly.

4. Place a bundle of herbs inside each hen's cavity. Cross the drumsticks in front of the cavities and secure with twine. Roast the hens in the oven for 15 minutes. Rotate the pan in the oven and roast for 10 more minutes. Baste the hens with the pan juices, and roast for another 10 to 15 minutes, or until golden brown on the outside and the juices run clear when the thigh is pierced. Remove from the oven, cut the twine, and remove the herbs from the cavities.

5. Cook the potatoes in a medium pot of boiling salted water until fork-tender, 10 to 15 minutes. Drain and run them through a ricer. Set aside in a large mixing bowl.

6. Open the bags with the livers and gizzards, and discard the gizzards (the hard pieces). Melt the butter with the livers in a medium saucepan over medium heat, and cook the livers, stirring occasionally, until browned, 3 to 5 minutes. Pour the cream into the saucepan and bring the mixture to a boil. Lower the heat and let the mixture simmer for 2 minutes. Remove the livers and cream from the heat and allow to cool for 5 minutes. Pour into a blender and blend for 20 to 30 seconds.

7. Slowly pour the blended cream mixture into the potatoes and mix until smooth. (You may not need to use all the cream to get the desired consistency.) Add the white truffle oil, season with salt and pepper, and mix well.

8. To serve, divide the herbs from the roasting pan among 4 dinner plates. Place 1 hen on each bed of herbs. Serve the potatoes next to the hens.

SKIRT STEAK WITH FLASH-SAUTÉED TOMATO AND BUFFALO MOZZARELLA SALAD

4 servings

My favorite thing about this dish is the tomato and buffalo mozzarella salad. Flash sautéing it is great because it softens the mozzarella and mellows the flavors of the tomatoes and vinaigrette just a bit. I also love how the warm salad just seeps into the meat, adding a fresh summery flavor to the dish.

For the salad:

2 cups halved yellow and red cherry tomatoes

¼ cup balsamic vinegar

⅓ cup extra-virgin olive oil

1 teaspoon sugar

1 teaspoon salt

Pinch of black pepper

2 tablespoons chopped fresh basil

1 tablespoon chopped fresh parsley

8 ounces buffalo mozzarella, cut into ¼-inch dice

For the steak:

2 pounds skirt steak, cut into 4 pieces

1 teaspoon salt

¼ teaspoon black pepper

3 tablespoon olive oil

(Continued)

1. Toss all the salad ingredients together in a large mixing bowl. Set aside at room temperature while you cook the steaks.

2. Gently pat the steaks dry with a paper towel. Sprinkle both sides with salt and pepper. Heat the olive oil in a heavy 12-inch skillet over high heat until it's hot, but not smoking. Add the steaks and cook for 4 minutes on each side.

3. While the steaks cook, place a medium sauté pan over medium heat. Allow the pan to get hot for 2 to 3 minutes. Pour the entire salad, including all the juices, into the pan and sauté for 30 seconds.

4. Remove the steaks from the pan and place on dinner plates. Immediately spoon the tomato salad over the steaks and serve.

RIB-EYE STEAK
WITH FINGERLING POTATOES

4 servings

*Rib-eye is my favorite cut of beef. It's well marbleized and therefore really tender
and flavorful. I think it's a no-brainer on the grill, pretty much foolproof.
Fingerling potatoes are, in my opinion, the perfect size. They're like
a cross between French fries and baked potatoes.*

For the fingerling potatoes:

1¾ to 2 pounds fingerling potatoes, cut lengthwise in quarters (do not peel)

2 tablespoons olive oil

2¼ teaspoons salt

1 teaspoon black pepper

4 sprigs fresh rosemary

15 sprigs fresh thyme

8 garlic cloves

For the steak:

Four 8- to 10-ounce rib-eye steaks, about 1 inch thick, trimmed of excess fat around edges

¼ cup olive oil

2 tablespoons salt

1 teaspoon black pepper

(Continued)

1. To cook the potatoes, preheat the oven to 350°F. In a large mixing bowl, combine all the ingredients. Lay the potatoes, skin side up, on a baking sheet. Bake in the oven for 30 minutes. The potatoes should be light golden brown and crispy. Remove from the oven.

2. To cook the steaks, prepare the grill. If you are using a gas grill, turn the burners on high and keep the grill covered for at least 10 minutes. If you are using a charcoal grill, wait until the fire is medium-hot (you should be able to hold your hand 6 inches above the rack for 3 to 4 seconds before pulling away).

3. While the grill is heating, put the steaks on a plate or work surface. Brush both sides of each steak with olive oil, and sprinkle both sides with salt and pepper. Let the steaks sit at room temperature until the grill is ready.

4. Place the steaks on the grill and cook for 4 to 5 minutes on one side. Flip the steaks over and cook for 3 to 4 minutes for medium-rare. Remove from the grill and allow them to rest for 3 to 4 minutes before slicing.

5. Divide the slices among 4 plates and serve the potatoes alongside the steak.

Eleven

FISH

SOY-AND-HONEY-GLAZED ARCTIC CHAR WITH POTATO AND CUCUMBER SALAD

4 servings

As I've said before, I love combining hot and cold elements on the same plate, and this dish is a great example. The chilled potato and cucumber salad is a refreshing and savory counterpart to the char, which takes on a sweet crust from the honey and soy. This dish didn't really fit on Ápizz's menu, so I served it at the Orchard as soon as we opened.

For the potato and cucumber salad:

2 potatoes, peeled and cut into ¼-inch cubes

2 tablespoons chopped green onion (white and light green parts)

2 tablespoons fresh lemon juice

3 tablespoons crème fraîche or sour cream

1½ teaspoons salt

Pinch of black pepper

1 tablespoon chopped fresh dill

2 cucumbers, peeled, cut in half lengthwise, cut into slices

(Continued)

For the Arctic char:
   ¼ cup honey
   2 teaspoons soy sauce
   4 Arctic char fillets, 6 to 7 ounces each
   2 tablespoons olive oil plus extra for rubbing the fish
   Salt and black pepper to taste

1. To begin the salad, cook the potatoes in a pot of boiling salted water until tender yet firm.

2. In a medium mixing bowl, combine the green onions, lemon juice, crème fraîche, salt, pepper, and dill. Toss in the potatoes and cucumbers and gently mix together. The salad should be refrigerated for at least 30 minutes and up to 2 hours before serving.

3. To make the fish, in a small mixing bowl, whisk together the honey and soy sauce. Set aside. Rub both sides of the char fillets with olive oil and sprinkle with salt and pepper. In a large sauté pan (big enough to hold all 4 fillets), heat the 2 tablespoons of olive oil over medium heat until it begins to shimmer. Add the fillets to the pan and sear until the bottom side begins to brown, 4 to 5 minutes. Flip the fish over and cook the other side until it is just opaque in the center, about 3 to 4 minutes. During the last minute of cooking, brush both sides of the fish with the honey and soy sauce mixture.

4. Transfer the fish to 4 dinner plates and brush the tops with another light coat of the honey and soy sauce mixture right before serving. Serve alongside the cold potato and cucumber salad.

FRIED FLOUNDER SALAD

4 servings

I came up with this dish because I love combining anything fried with a salad. I like the way the flavors of the salad—especially the vinaigrette and the juices from the tomatoes— seep into the breading of whatever is fried. The classic Italian dish veal Milanese, which is a breaded veal chop topped with a green salad, is a great example of how simple and beautiful the combination can be. This fish recipe is my riff on that idea.

For the flounder:

2 large eggs

¼ cup milk

1 cup all-purpose flour

3 cups Herbed Bread Crumbs (page 195)

4 flounder fillets, 6 to 8 ounces each

1 teaspoon salt

½ teaspoon black pepper

¼ cup olive oil

For the salad:

¼ cup olive oil

1 tablespoon fresh lemon juice

½ teaspoon sugar

½ teaspoon salt

Pinch of black pepper

1 tablespoon diced red onion

4 cups baby arugula

2 cups halved yellow and red cherry tomatoes

To serve:

2 tablespoons crème fraîche

1 lemon, cut into quarters

(Continued)

1. To make the flounder, in a shallow bowl, whisk together the eggs and milk. Spread out the flour on a plate. Spread out the bread crumbs on a separate plate. Sprinkle both sides of the fish fillets with salt and pepper. Dredge each fillet in the flour, shaking off any excess flour, and dip into the bowl of whisked eggs. Finally, coat each fillet with bread crumbs.

2. Heat the olive oil in a large, heavy skillet over medium-high heat until it begins to smoke. Add the fillets and cook until the coating is golden brown and the fillets are opaque in the center, about 3 minutes per side.

3. To make the salad, in a medium mixing bowl, whisk together the salad dressing ingredients. Add the arugula and cherry tomatoes and toss well to coat.

4. To serve, divide the salad among 4 dinner plates. Lay 1 fried fillet over each salad, add a dollop of crème fraîche in the center of each fillet and place a lemon quarter alongside.

GLAZED SALMON AND BEAN SALAD

4 servings

This recipe was inspired by some of the dishes the guys in my kitchen make for staff meals. There's a lot going on in the bean salad, and its intense flavors offset the sweetness of the salmon glaze.

For the glaze:

¼ cup honey

1 teaspoon Worcestershire sauce

For the bean salad:

One 18-ounce can black beans

One 18-ounce can cannellini beans

¼ cup diced celery

¼ cup diced carrots

2 tablespoons chopped red onion

2 tablespoons crème fraîche

1 teaspoon fresh lemon juice

1 tablespoon balsamic vinegar

1 teaspoon salt

1 teaspoon sugar

1 tablespoon chopped fresh basil

1 tablespoon chopped fresh parsley

1 tablespoon chopped fresh cilantro

For the salmon:

4 salmon fillets, about 6 ounces each, skin removed

Salt and black pepper to taste

2 tablespoons olive oil

(Continued)

1. To make the glaze, combine the honey and Worcestershire sauce in a small mixing bowl. Set aside.

2. To make the bean salad, combine all the ingredients in a large mixing bowl. Let the salad stand at room temperature for at least 15 minutes to allow the flavors to blend.

3. To make the salmon, sprinkle the fillets with salt and pepper on both sides. Heat the olive oil in a 12-inch sauté pan over medium heat until it begins to shimmer. Add the salmon to the pan and cook for 4 to 5 minutes on each side. During the last minute, brush each side liberally with the glaze.

4. Divide the bean salad among 4 dinner plates. Place 1 salmon fillet on top of each plate of bean salad. Serve immediately.

GRILLED SALMON WITH BASIL-DIJON BUTTER

6 servings

This dish reminds me of summer because when it's hot outside, dinner is all about the grill. The simplicity of this recipe will make even the beginner cook look good—all it takes is fresh fish and great herbs (some corn on the cob wouldn't hurt, either). A no-brainer.

¼ cup fresh chopped parsley

½ cup fresh chopped basil

1 stick (½ cup) butter at room temperature

1 tablespoon diced shallots

1 tablespoon Dijon mustard

1 teaspoon salt plus extra for seasoning the fish

Pinch of black pepper plus extra for seasoning the fish

Six 6-ounce salmon steaks, 1 inch thick

(Continued)

1. Prepare the grill for cooking. If you are using a gas grill, turn the burners on high and keep the grill covered for at least 10 minutes. If you are using a charcoal grill, wait until the fire is medium-hot (you should be able to hold your hand 6 inches above the rack for 3 to 4 seconds before pulling away).

2. In a large mixing bowl, combine the parsley, basil, butter, shallots, mustard, 1 teaspoon of salt, and the pinch of pepper. Refrigerate the mixture for up to 30 minutes.

3. Season the salmon steaks with salt and pepper. Rub a generous amount of the basil-Dijon-butter mixture on one side of each steak. Place the salmon on the grill, buttered side up, and cook 4 to 5 minutes. Turn the salmon over and, and with a brush or spoon, spread the rest of the butter mixture on the salmon. Cook for 4 to 5 minutes more, or until the center of the fish is opaque.

OVEN-BAKED SKATE WITH ROASTED ROSEMARY POTATOES

4 servings

This is one of the most intensely flavorful dishes on the menu at Ápizz, thanks to the olives and capers, which sizzle over the fish. At Ápizz we serve this dish with crispy rosemary potatoes, but the dish also goes well with a fresh green salad or wilted baby spinach.

For the potatoes:

2 baking potatoes, sliced into 1/8-inch disks

1 tablespoon salt

2 tablespoons olive oil

Pinch of black pepper

3 garlic cloves

3 sprigs fresh rosemary

For the skate:

Four 6-ounce skate fillets

1/4 cup dry white wine

1/4 cup fresh lemon juice

4 teaspoons capers, drained

4 large green Spanish olives, pitted and sliced

4 teaspoons salt

4 pinches of black pepper

1/2 cup olive oil

1/4 cup Herbed Bread Crumbs (page 195)

2 tablespoons butter plus extra for greasing the baking dish

1/2 lemon, sliced

(Continued)

1. To make the potatoes, preheat the oven to 375°F. Combine all the ingredients in a medium mixing bowl. Place on a baking sheet, including the garlic and rosemary branches. Bake the potatoes until they are golden brown, 30 to 40 minutes. Remove the baking sheet from the oven, cover with aluminum foil to retain the heat, and set aside.

2. To make the fish, raise the oven temperature to 400°F. Grease the bottom of a medium to large ovenproof casserole dish with butter. Cover the bottom of the dish with the skate fillets without overlapping them. Cover the fish with the white wine and lemon juice. Scatter the capers and olives over the skate fillets and sprinkle with salt and pepper. Pour the olive oil over the fish and sprinkle evenly with the bread crumbs. Place 1½ teaspoons of butter on top of each fillet. Bake the fish for 10 minutes, put a slice of lemon on top of each fillet, and bake for 8 to 10 minutes more, or until the fish is opaque and the bread crumbs are browned. Five minutes before the skate is finished, put the potatoes, uncovered, back in the oven to reheat.

3. Divide the skate fillets among four dinner plates. Arrange the potato slices along the edge of each fillet and serve.

OVEN-ROASTED
WHOLE STRIPED BASS

4 servings

*This recipe looks simple, and it is, but it is consistently a bestseller at Ápizz.
We tried to take it off the menu for a couple of weeks, but had to bring it back by
popular demand. Since the fish is roasted whole in the oven, it retains all of its
juices and flavor. Some people like it filleted, but most prefer it sprawled
across their plate, head and tail intact.*

4 whole striped bass, 1¼ to 1½ pounds each, gutted and cleaned

1 lemon, thinly sliced

4 sprigs fresh rosemary

4 sprigs fresh thyme

6 tablespoons salt

1 tablespoon black pepper plus extra for the cavity

1 to 1⅓ cups olive oil

1. Preheat the oven to 400°F. Place each fish in an individual terra-cotta or casserole dish. Using your fingers to gently pry open the body of each fish, stuff each one with 2 slices of lemon, 1 sprig of rosemary, 1 sprig of thyme, 1½ teaspoons of salt, and a pinch of pepper. Close each fish.

2. Use ¼ to ⅓ cup of olive oil to evenly coat the skin on both sides of each fish. Sprinkle the remaining 1 tablespoon of salt and ¾ teaspoon of pepper on each fish (half on each side).

3. Bake the fish for 25 minutes, or until the skin is crispy on the outside and the meat is opaque, tender, and juicy on the inside. Remove the dishes from the oven and serve the fish whole.

STRIPED BASS POACHED
WITH TOMATOES

4 servings

*Poaching the bass allows it to absorb the beautiful flavors of the basil, mint,
and parsley. This is a very light, delicate dish and goes well
with a heartier side like potatoes or risotto.*

4 tablespoons olive oil

1 onion, thinly sliced

4 slices bacon, cut crosswise into ½-inch pieces

1 tablespoon chopped garlic

½ cup dry white wine

One 28-ounce can crushed plum tomatoes

1½ cups Vegetable Stock (page 196)

1 tablespoon chopped fresh basil

1 tablespoon chopped fresh mint

1 tablespoon chopped fresh parsley

2 teaspoons salt

½ teaspoon black pepper

4 striped bass fillets with skin, 6 to 7 ounces each

2 tablespoon butter

1 lemon cut into quarters

1. Preheat the oven to 325°F. Heat 2 tablespoons of the olive oil with the onion and bacon in a medium saucepan over medium heat. Cook until the onions soften and the bacon turns golden, about 6 minutes. Add the garlic and cook for 1 minute. Add the wine and cook for an additional minute. Add the tomatoes (including juice), vegetable stock, basil, mint, parsley, 1 teaspoon of the salt, and ¼ teaspoon of the pepper and simmer, uncovered, for 3 minutes.

2. Meanwhile, pat the bass fillets dry with a paper towel. Sprinkle the fish with the remaining 1 teaspoon of salt and ¼ teaspoon of pepper.

3. Transfer the sauce to a 3-quart glass or ceramic baking dish, about 13 x 9 x 2 inches. Arrange the fish over the sauce. Top with the butter and lemon slices. Cover the dish tightly with aluminum foil and bake just until the fish is opaque and cooked through, 14 to 16 minutes. Remove the baking dish from the oven and let the fish rest in the dish, covered, for 3 minutes, as it will steam more and the flavors will intensify.

Twelve

BASIC RECIPES

THIS CHAPTER INCLUDES my basic, go-to recipes—the ones I turn to over and over again to liven up a salad, make a pizza, or inject some flavor into risotto. Feel free to experiment with how you use some of these, especially the salad dressings. The Red Wine and Dijon Mustard Vinaigrette (page 194), for example, is great when drizzled over meat in an Italian hero. The Basic Tomato Sauce (page 197) can be tossed with a simple pasta dish, spooned onto a pizza, or dolloped on a piece of crispy bruschetta.

CREAMY RED WINE VINAIGRETTE

2¼ cups

½ cup extra-virgin olive oil
¾ cup heavy cream
¼ cup red wine vinegar
1 tablespoon chopped shallots
2 tablespoons sugar
1 tablespoon salt
1 tablespoon fresh lemon juice
1 tablespoon Dijon mustard

In a small to medium mixing bowl, whisk together all the ingredients. The dressing can be stored in the refrigerator in a covered jar for up to 3 days.

RED WINE AND DIJON MUSTARD VINAIGRETTE

3¾ cups

2 cups extra-virgin olive oil
1 cup red wine vinegar
2 tablespoons chopped shallots
3 tablespoons sugar
2 tablespoons salt
2 tablespoons fresh lemon juice
2 tablespoons Dijon mustard
¾ teaspoon black pepper

In a medium mixing bowl, whisk together all the ingredients. The dressing can be stored in the refrigerator in a covered jar for up to 1 week. Shake the jar vigorously before pouring.

LEMON-HONEY VINAIGRETTE

2¼ cups

1 cup extra-virgin olive oil
½ cup fresh lemon juice
½ cup white vinegar
½ cup honey
1 shallot, chopped
1 teaspoon salt
½ teaspoon freshly ground black pepper

In a small to medium mixing bowl, whisk together all the ingredients. The dressing can be stored in the refrigerator in a covered jar for up to 1 week. Shake the jar vigorously before pouring.

HERBED BREAD CRUMBS

2½ cups

1 tablespoon chopped fresh rosemary
¼ cup grated Parmigiano-Reggiano cheese
2 cups plain bread crumbs
1 tablespoon chopped fresh thyme
1 tablespoon chopped fresh parsley
1 tablespoon minced garlic
3 tablespoons extra-virgin olive oil
1 tablespoon salt
Pinch of black pepper

In a medium mixing bowl, combine all the ingredients. Cover the bowl with plastic wrap and store in the refrigerator for up to 10 days.

VEGETABLE STOCK

6 cups

1 carrot, roughly chopped
2 celery stalks, roughly chopped
1 large onion, roughly chopped
2 tablespoons salt

1. Heat 8 cups of water in a medium stockpot over high heat. Right before the water begins to boil, add the carrot, celery, onion, and salt. Bring the liquid to a boil and reduce the heat slightly so the liquid remains at a gentle boil. Continue boiling for 30 minutes.

2. Remove the pot from the heat and strain the liquid, discarding all the vegetables. The stock can be stored, covered, in the refrigerator for up to 1 week, or in the freezer for up to 3 months.

BASIC TOMATO SAUCE

5 to 6 cups

¼ cup chopped shallots

1 tablespoon chopped garlic

¼ cup olive oil

Two 28-ounce cans whole plum tomatoes

1 teaspoon dried oregano

2 tablespoons salt

Pinch of black pepper

Pinch of crushed red pepper (optional)

1. In a large stockpot over medium heat, cook the shallots and garlic in the oil until they soften, 6 to 8 minutes. Add the tomatoes, oregano, salt, black pepper, red pepper, and ½ cup of water.

2. Raise the heat to high and cook for 30 minutes, stirring occasionally and breaking up the tomatoes slightly with a wooden spoon. Lower the heat to medium and simmer for 30 to 45 minutes. The sauce can be stored in the freezer in an airtight container for up to 3 months.

PREBAKED PIZZA CRUST

Five 12 × 6 inch pizzas

½ teaspoon active dry yeast

3½ cups all-purpose flour plus extra for kneading

2 tablespoons plus 2 teaspoons salt

2 tablespoons plus 2 teaspoons olive oil

1. In a small mixing bowl, stir together 1 cup of warm water (about 110°F) and the yeast. In a food processor, combine 1 cup of the flour, the salt, and 2 tablespoons of the olive oil. Add the yeast mixture and an additional 1½ cups of flour and process until well blended. Add the remaining flour and 2 tablespoons cold water and process for 1 minute more.

2. Transfer the dough to a lightly floured surface and knead for several minutes, until the dough is a smooth round ball. Rub 1 teaspoon of olive oil onto the top side of the ball, using your fingers to coat the surface evenly. Flip the dough over and repeat the process with the remaining teaspoon of olive oil. Place a lightly dampened kitchen towel over the dough and allow it to rise at room temperature for 1 hour until dough is close to double in size.

3. Divide the dough into five 5-ounce balls, about the size of a tennis ball. Preheat the oven to 350°F. Working with one ball of dough at a time, use your fingers to pat the dough into a rectangle measuring about 6 × 3 inches. With a floured rolling pin, roll the dough to stretch it in all directions, adding additional flour when necessary, until the crust is about ⅛ inch thin, 12 inches long, and 6 inches wide. Gently pull the corners in an outward direction to maintain the crust's rectangular shape.

4. Bake the dough on a pizza stone or directly on an oven rack for 4 to 5 minutes, or until the dough is lightly browned. Remove the dough from the oven and cool to room temperature. You can wrap the prebaked dough with plastic wrap and store in the refrigerator for 2 to 3 days, or in the freezer for 1 week, or use immediately. For pizza recipes, see pages 106 to 107.

PIZZA SAUCE

3 to 4 cups

Two 28-ounce cans whole plum tomatoes
1 teaspoon minced garlic
2 tablespoons extra-virgin olive oil
1 tablespoon salt
1 tablespoon chopped basil

Drain the tomatoes well. Put them on a cutting board and dice into ¼-inch pieces. Transfer to a medium mixing bowl and add the remaining ingredients. The mixture can be stored in a covered container in the refrigerator for 2 to 3 days, or used immediately on top of the pizza.

Thirteen

DESSERTS

APPLE CRUMBLE

6 servings

*I fell in love with this dessert when I first baked it at our summer house near the beach.
The humidity out by the ocean gave the crumble this amazing moistness,
which can be difficult to replicate. Even though I make it every
Fourth of July, it's really the perfect dessert for the
fall months and Thanksgiving.*

3 cups peeled, cored, and diced Granny Smith apples

1 teaspoon cinnamon

½ teaspoon salt

1 tablespoon lemon juice

1 tablespoon cornstarch

½ cup Quaker Maple and Brown Sugar Oatmeal

¾ cup all-purpose flour

¾ cup brown sugar

1 stick butter

Vanilla gelato for serving

(Continued)

1. Preheat the oven to 350°F. Place the apples in a large bowl and sprinkle with the cinnamon, salt, lemon juice, cornstarch, oatmeal, and ¼ cup of water. Set aside.

2. In a separate medium bowl, mix together the flour and brown sugar. Cut in the butter with a table knife and mix with both hands until crumbly. Mix half of the crumble with the apples.

3. Divide the apple-and-crumble mixture among 6 ramekins, 4 inches in diameter and 1 inch deep. Sprinkle some of the extra crumble on top of each ramekin to cover. Bake the ramekins until the crumble browns slightly, 20 to 25 minutes. Serve immediately with a scoop of vanilla gelato.

BANANA NUT BREAD

1 loaf

*I started playing around with this recipe when I thought I would serve brunch at Ápizz.
I loved the idea of putting a basket of warm banana nut bread on the table as
soon as people sat down. Though I chose to blow off brunch, I still
make this recipe at home from time to time. We eat it warm
with jam for breakfast or pick on it late
at night in front of the television.*

1 cup all-purpose flour plus extra for dusting pan

⅛ teaspoon baking powder

1 stick (½ cup) unsalted butter at room temperature plus extra for greasing pan

1½ tablespoons vegetable oil

¾ cup sugar

4 large eggs

2 ripe medium bananas, peeled and mashed

1 teaspoon vanilla extract

½ cup chopped walnuts

(Continued)

1. Preheat the oven to 325°F. Butter an 8½ × 4½ × 2½-inch loaf pan. Dust the pan with flour, tapping out the excess. Sift together the flour and baking powder into a small mixing bowl. Set aside.

2. Using an electric mixer fitted with a paddle attachment, mix together the butter, oil, and sugar at low speed. Increase the speed to medium and add the eggs one at a time, beating well after each addition. Mix in the mashed bananas, vanilla, and nuts. Add the flour mixture and mix until the batter is smooth. Pour the batter into the buttered pan, smoothing the top with a large spoon or spatula.

3. Bake the bread in the oven until the top is golden brown, 55 to 60 minutes, or until a toothpick inserted in the center comes out clean. Cool the bread in the pan on a wire rack for 15 minutes. Unmold the bread and let it cool completely on the rack. The bread can be stored in an airtight container at room temperature for up to 4 days, or in the freezer (wrapped in aluminum foil) for up to 1 month.

FRESH PEACHES IN RED WINE REDUCTION

4 servings

This refreshing dessert reminds my wife of sitting at a beachside restaurant in Capri, Italy. It brings to my mind a leisurely moment at a tiny sidewalk table on Mulberry Street in Little Italy. Wherever you intend to enjoy it, use the ripest peaches you can find. On the other hand, if your peaches are less than perfect, you'll be so buzzed after a couple of servings, you won't even notice.

2 cups red wine

2 cups sugar

4 peaches, pitted and cut into quarters

½ cup fresh lemon juice

1. Heat the wine and sugar in a medium saucepan over medium heat until all the sugar is dissolved. Lower the heat slightly and simmer for 8 to 10 minutes, until the mixture becomes slightly syrupy.

2. Place the peaches in a medium mixing bowl and stir in the wine and lemon juice. Cover the bowl with plastic wrap and refrigerate for up to 24 hours. Serve in small dessert bowls or wine glasses.

CREAMSICLE PANNA COTTA

4 servings

This is my wife's favorite dessert at Ápizz. She says it's so light that no matter how full she is—and she can eat—she always finds room for it. Panna cotta is traditionally eaten plain, but I wanted to come up with a more original version. The frozen creamsicle on a stick that I used to buy from the ice cream truck in Canarsie was my inspiration for the recipe.

1¼ teaspoons unflavored gelatin

½ cup store-bought orange juice

½ cup sugar

2 cups heavy cream

1 teaspoon vanilla extract

Zest of ¼ orange

1 drop orange food coloring (optional)

16 mandarin orange wedges (one 12-ounce can or 2 whole fresh mandarin oranges)

1. Combine the gelatin and 2 tablespoons water in a small bowl. Allow the mixture to sit for 15 minutes, or until the gelatin dissolves.

2. In a small saucepan over low heat, combine the orange juice with 2 tablespoons of the sugar. Simmer the liquid until reduced to ¼ cup. Set the mixture aside.

3. In a medium saucepan over medium heat, whisk together the cream, remaining 6 tablespoons of sugar, the vanilla, and orange zest until the liquid comes to a low simmer.

4. Add the softened gelatin and stir well. Whisk in the reduced orange juice and remove the mixture from the heat. Let sit for 15 minutes to cool.

5. Pour the mixture through a strainer into a large measuring cup or medium bowl to remove the orange zest. Add the food coloring, if using, and stir well.

6. Lightly coat four 3-inch ramekins or teacups with a nonstick cooking spray. Pour ½ cup of the panna cotta into each ramekin and refrigerate, uncovered, for 4 hours.

7. To serve, unmold each panna cotta by gently running a butter knife around its edge and shaking it out, upside down, onto a serving plate. Garnish with 4 mandarin orange wedges.

MASCARPONE CHEESECAKE

8 servings

*When it's done right, there are few desserts better than cheesecake.
This one is a big hit at Ápizz; the addition of mascarpone mellows
the cream cheese a bit and makes it somewhat Italian!*

6 tablespoons unsalted butter

2 cups graham cracker crumbs

1 pound cream cheese, at room temperature

1 cup sugar

¼ cup cornstarch

8 ounces mascarpone, at room temperature

½ cup heavy cream

¼ teaspoon vanilla extract

2 extra-large eggs, at room temperature

Sliced fresh strawberries for serving

1. Preheat the oven to 300°F. To make the crust, in a small sauté pan over low heat, melt the butter. In a medium mixing bowl, combine the melted butter with the graham cracker crumbs, mixing well with your hands. Set aside.

2. Line the bottom of a 9-inch springform pan with parchment paper. Lay one sheet of aluminum foil, slightly larger than the pan, on a work surface and place the pan in the center of the foil. Curl up the foil around the pan so it comes up about halfway. Spray the pan with a nonstick cooking spray. Pat the buttered graham cracker crumbs onto the bottom and ½ inch up the sides of the pan.

3. In a medium mixing bowl, combine 4 ounces of the cream cheese, ½ cup of the sugar, and the cornstarch in the bowl of an electric mixer. Beat on low until the mixture is creamy, 3 to 4 minutes. Beat in the remaining 12 ounces of cream cheese, mixing well until the mixture is smooth. Add the mascarpone in 2 batches, continuing to beat the mixture until it's smooth. Add in the remaining ½ cup of sugar, the heavy cream, and vanilla extract, one at a time, beating well after each ingredient is added. Beat in the eggs one at a time, and continue beating until the mixture is smooth.

4. Pour the mixture into the pan. Run a butter knife between the crust and the sides of the pan before baking. Place the pan in a larger baking pan. Fill the larger pan with enough water to come about halfway up the smaller pan. Place the pans in the oven and bake for 35 to 40 minutes, or until the center of the cheesecake barely jiggles. Allow the cheesecake to cool on a wire rack for 20 minutes, then refrigerate in the pan for 1 hour. Release the sides of the pan and serve with fresh strawberries.

WHITE CHOCOLATE
BREAD PUDDING

6 servings

This is a decadent, rich dessert that's amazing when served warm with gelato. What's different about this version of bread pudding—and, in my opinion, what makes it so good—is that it calls for Italian bread instead of the usual French brioche. At Ápizz, we use filone, *a delicious, crusty bread found in most good Italian bakeries.*

10 ounces chopped white chocolate

3 bananas, chopped into 1-inch pieces

⅓ cup plus ¼ cup milk

1 loaf day-old *filone* bread or any seedless Italian bread, crust removed, and cut into 1-inch
   cubes (about 8 cups)

1 tablespoon cinnamon

1 cup heavy cream

1½ cups sugar

1½ teaspoons vanilla extract

2 large eggs

1. Preheat the oven to 325°F. Lightly spray six 4-inch ramekins with a nonstick cooking spray.

2. Melt the white chocolate in the top of a double boiler over lightly simmering water, stirring occasionally. Set the chocolate aside and let it cool to lukewarm.

3. While the chocolate is melting, combine the bananas and ¼ cup of the milk in a blender and puree for 1 to 2 minutes. You should have 1¼ to 1½ cups of banana puree.

4. Put the bread in a medium mixing bowl, dust with the cinnamon, and set aside.

5. In a medium saucepan over medium heat, warm the cream and remaining ⅓ cup of milk. Add the sugar, stirring until it is dissolved. Stir in the vanilla, half of the melted white chocolate, and the banana puree. Reduce the heat slightly and let the mixture simmer uncovered.

6. Whisk the eggs in a small bowl. Temper the eggs by slowly whisking in ¼ cup of the heated cream and banana puree. Slowly pour the tempered eggs into the saucepan with the cream and banana puree, whisking the mixture as you pour.

7. Pour the custard over the bread, mixing it well to coat the bread. Pour the bread mixture into the 6 ramekins, packing each ramekin tightly to form an even surface. With a small spatula or butter knife, spread a thin layer of the remaining white chocolate over the surface of each bread pudding. Cover each ramekin with aluminum foil and bake for 30 minutes. Remove the aluminum foil and bake the bread puddings for an additional 10 to 15 minutes, or until the tops are golden brown.

ACKNOWLEDGMENTS

SPECIAL THANKS TO Judith Regan for having a huge pair of meatballs in taking a shot with me. I'm grateful and will never forget it.

To Paul Fedorko, my agent, for being one of the few people I have met who delivers on a promise. Thank you for having my back.

To Cassie Jones, our editor at Regan, for encouraging us to keep it real and guiding us along the way, and to the other great people on the Regan team: Jessica Di Biase, Adrienne Makowski, Richard Ljoenes, Lawrence Pekarek, and Jennifer Brunn.

To Jim Mannino, for putting this whole thing together. Thank you for turning down money, opting instead to receive sexual favors.

To Mario Cantone and Jerry Dixon for your support, friendship, and of course, for making us laugh our asses off along the way.

Pam and I would like to extend our gratitude to Jennifer Belle. Thanks for your invaluable input, advice, and editing, and for listening to countless rewrites of the same chapters. Special thanks to Jessica Olshen for reading drafts, testing recipes, and being a great friend. Thank you Mary Billard for your insight, advice, and support. To Deborah A. Riley, thank you for all your hard work on last-minute editing.

Special thanks to Xerxes Novoa ("X") for always being two steps ahead of everyone else. I could not run these restaurants without you.

To Elizabeth Watt, photographer, for using her kick-ass talent to make my food look great.

To Jim "Great Neck" Richman and Leon Wagner, thank you for believing in me and changing my life with one phone call.

To my kitchen staff at Ápizz and the Orchard: Lorenzo Marroquin, Marco Antonio Toledo, Diego Castillo, Narciso Aldana, Omar Torres de la Rosa, Santos Marroquin, Diego Gutierrez, Eulalio Aldana, Miguel Torres, Sergio Juarez, Manuel Casarrubias, Angel and Carmen Paredes, Arturo Torres, and Jose Perez. You guys are the backbone of the restaurants. Thank you for your hard work and loyalty.

Thanks to Pam's mom, Elaine Manela, and sister, Marci Sanft, for their help in reading early drafts. Thank you to Eleanor Pilgrim for making our lives so much easier. We love you.

Special thanks to my sister, Flora LaFemina, and my parents, Joseph and Rose LaFemina, for your unconditional love, support, and encouragement. Mom, thank you for cooking great meals all my life and cultivating my love for food, and for finally sharing your eggplant recipe with the world. I love you all.

And finally, thank you to all of my diners. My restaurants would not exist without you.

INDEX

cream, heavy (*continued*)

    in porcini mushroom and white truffle oil soup, 119–20

    in potatoes, for roasted Cornish hens, 173–74

    in red pepper and fresh basil soup with crispy shallots, 123–25

    in roasted chestnut soup, 121–22

    -tomato sauce, pappardelle with lobster tail in, 142–43

    tomato sauce, rigatoni with sweet Italian sausage and, 156–57

    in white chocolate bread pudding, 210–11

cream cheese, in mascarpone cheesecake, 208–9

creamsicle panna cotta, 206–7

crème fraîche:

    in bean salad, glazed salmon with, 183–84

    in lentil, crispy pancetta, and wilted arugula soup, 117–18

    in potato and cucumber salad, soy-and-honey-glazed Arctic char with, 179–80

    salmon tartare with potato crisps and red onion, 102–3

crostini, buffalo mozzarella, tomato, and anchovy, 105

croutons, drunken goat cheese salad with red wine vinaigrette and, 130–31

cucumber and potato salad, soy-and-honey-glazed Arctic char with, 179–80

Culinary Institute of America, 57

Daily Candy, 64–65, 70–71

Dean & Deluca, 76

DeCarlo, Frank, 8–11, 60

desserts, 201–11

    apple crumble, 201–2

    banana nut bread, 203–4

creamsicle panna cotta, 206–7

    fresh peaches in red wine reduction, 205

    mascarpone cheesecake, 208–9

    white chocolate bread pudding, 210–11

Diego (bartender), 71

Dijon mustard:

    -basil butter, grilled salmon with, 185–86

    in berry chutney, 92–93

    in red wine vinaigrette, 194

"Diner's Journal" (Asimov), 72–73

drunken goat cheese salad with croutons and red wine vinaigrette, 130–31

East Village, New York, N.Y., 9, 11, 28

eggplant, Mom's, in tomato sauce, 108–9

eggs:

    in banana nut bread, 203–4

    in basic gnocchi, 151–52

    in fried flounder salad, 181–82

    in mascarpone cheesecake, 208–9

    in Mom's eggplant in tomato sauce, 108–9

    in white chocolate bread pudding, 210–11

Eldridge Street, New York, N.Y., 3–4, 13, 21–24, 30, 59, 61, 71

Fabricant, Florence, 61, 70

farfalle with green beans, potatoes, and pesto, 163–64

fennel, mixed greens with orange, pink grapefruit and, 136

fish, 179–91

    fried flounder salad, 181–82

    glazed salmon and bean salad, 182–83

    grilled salmon with basil-Dijon butter, 185–86

oven-baked skate with roasted rosemary
potatoes, 187–88
oven-roasted whole striped bass, 189
salmon tartare with potato crisps and red
onion crème fraîche, 102–3
soy-and-honey-glazed Arctic char with
potato and cucumber salad, 179–80
striped bass poached with tomatoes, 190–91
flounder, fried, salad, 181–82

garlic chips, crispy, shrimp and chorizo with,
90–91
Gina (customer), 15
glaze(s):
balsamic, lentils with oven-roasted plum
tomatoes and, 96–97
port, pear and prosciutto salad with herbed
walnuts and, 134–35
gnocchi, 151–55
basic, 151–52
with honey-braised short ribs, 153–54
with tomato, black olive, and basil sauce,
155
Good Fellas, 40
green beans:
farfalle with potatoes, pesto and, 163–64
French, and Parmesan soup, 115–16
French, sautéed with tomatoes and basil,
87
greens:
mixed, with fennel, orange, and pink
grapefruit, 136
red leaf lettuce, in The Orchard salad,
132–33
romaine hearts, for drunken goat cheese
salad with croutons, and creamy red wine
vinaigrette, 130–31
see also arugula

herbed walnuts, 134–35
honey:
-braised short ribs, gnocchi with, 153–54
in chestnut cream sauce, sweet potato
agnolotti with, 160–62
cream, butternut squash soup with, 113–14
in glazed salmon and bean salad, 183–84
-lemon vinaigrette, 195
in roasted chestnut soup, 121–22
-and-soy-glazed Arctic char with potato and
cucumber salad, 179–80

Ian (head chef), 56–57, 63–65

José (busboy), 71

Lafemina, John:
on being a chef, 75–81
and OCD, 49–54
on owning a restaurant, 5–8
personal history of, 8–15
on real estate brokers, 17–21
on testing meatballs, 66–70
on work crews, 24–33
Lafemina, Pam Manela, 11–13, 15, 22–24,
49–50, 52–54, 60–62, 64–65, 67–68,
72–73, 77, 80
lamb, sliced tenderloin, with mint orzo,
171–72
lasagna with braised short ribs, 158–59
leek and pea risotto, 147–48
lemon:
cherry tomato, and bacon salad, 127–28
in cured beef tenderloin, 100–101
in fresh peaches in red wine reduction, 205
-honey vinaigrette, 195

prosciutto:

crispy, cherry tomato and potato salad with mustard vinaigrette and, 99

and pear salad with port glaze and herbed walnuts, 134–35

public relations, restaurants and, 60–65

Quang (contractor), 29–33, 39, 45, 49, 54, 57, 70

raisins, in The Orchard salad, 132–33

ravioli, open, with roasted butternut squash, 137–39

Ray (demolition worker), 27–28

red wine:

in braised chicken and potatoes in tomato sauce, 167–68

in cured beef tenderloin, 100–101

in honey-braised short ribs, gnocchi with, 153–54

in lasagna with braised short ribs, 158–59

reduction, fresh peaches in, 205

restaurant management, *see* Ápizz restaurant

rice, *see* risotto

ricotta cheese:

filling, veal, beef, and pork meatballs with, 169–70

in open ravioli with roasted butternut squash, 137–39

in pizza bianca, 107

rigatoni with sweet Italian sausage and tomato cream sauce, 156–57

risotto, 146–50

basic, 146

leek and pea, 147–48

mushroom, 149–50

rosemary roasted potatoes, oven-baked skate with, 187–88

Rosensweig's Lumber, Bronx, N.Y., 44–45

Rubenstein, Hal, 80

Rudy (consulting chef), 55–58, 75

salads, 127–36

arugula and soppressata, 129

cherry tomato, bacon, and lemon, 127–28

cherry tomato and potato, with crispy prosciutto and mustard vinaigrette, 99

drunken goat cheese, with croutons and creamy red wine vinaigrette, 130–31

flash-sautéed tomato and buffalo mozzarella, skirt steak with, 175–76

fried flounder, 181–82

glazed salmon and bean, 183–84

mixed greens with fennel, orange, and pink grapefruit, 136

The Orchard, 132–33

pear and prosciutto, with port glaze and herbed walnuts, 134–35

potato and cucumber, soy-and-honey-glazed Arctic char with, 179–80

salmon:

glazed, and bean salad, 183–84

grilled, with basil-Dijon butter 185–86

tartare with potato crisps and red onion crème fraîche, 102–3

Satin, Bobby, 10

sauces:

basic pizza, 199

basic tomato, 197

chestnut cream, sweet potato agnolotti with, 160–62

pesto, farfalle with green beans, potatoes and, 163–64

flash-sautéed, and buffalo mozzarella salad, skirt steak with, 175–76

French green beans sautéed with basil and, 87

in honey-braised short ribs, gnocchi with, 153–54

in lasagna with braised short ribs, 158–59

marinated, 94

oven-roasted plum, 98

oven-roasted plum, lentils with balsamic glaze and, 96–98

sauce, braised-chicken and potatoes in tomato sauce, 167–68

in steamed clams with chorizo, 88–89

striped bass poached with, 190–91

Uri ("design consultant"), 45, 48

veal, beef, and pork meatballs with ricotta filling, 169–70

vegetable stock, 196

vinaigrettes:
creamy red wine, 194
lemon-honey, 195
red wine and Dijon mustard, 194

Vincent (excavator), 32

walnuts:
in banana nut bread, 203–4
in The Orchard salad, 132–33
pear and prosciutto salad with port glaze and herbed, 134–35
in pesto, farfalle with green beans, potatoes and, 163–64

white chocolate bread pudding, 210–11

white truffle oil and porcini mushroom soup, 119–20

white wine:
in basic risotto, 146
in steamed clams with chorizo, 88–89
in striped bass poached with tomatoes, 190–91

Whole Foods market, 6, 80–81

HarperCollins books may be purchased for educational, business, or sales promotional use. For information please write: Special Markets Department, HarperCollins Publishers Inc., 10 East 53rd Street, New York, NY 10022.

FIRST EDITION

Designed by Judith Stagnitto Abbate and Richard Ljoenes

Printed on acid-free paper
Library of Congress Cataloging-in-Publication Data has been applied for.

ISBN 10: 0-06-085335-2
ISBN 13: 978-0-06-085335-8

06 07 08 09 10 RRD 10 9 8 7 6 5 4 3 2 1

I'd love to see you at my restaurants!

ÁPIZZ
217 Eldridge Street
New York, NY 10002
(212) 253-9199

ORCHARD
162 Orchard Street
New York, NY 10002
(212) 353-3570

PEASANT
194 Elizabeth Street
New York, NY 10012
(212) 965-9511